REVIEW
LATIN GRAMMAR

REVIEW
LATIN GRAMMAR

JOHN K. COLBY

Longman
New York & London

PREFACE

Many pupils emerge from their first year of Latin study with a weak grammatical foundation. As a result of this they often have serious trouble in the succeeding years of their Latin study. Unless definite steps are taken early to correct this deficiency, success in the second year and often in later years is usually difficult, often impossible to attain. At best every Latin student needs a thorough review of syntax before embarking upon the troublesome waters of second year translation, for his ability to translate Latin readily and correctly is many times directly dependent upon his knowledge of the elements of Latin syntax. Review Latin Grammar carefully studied will provide any student with the necessary grammatical foundation to insure his success in handling the work of the second and much of the later years of the Latin course.

GRAMMATICAL CONTENT: Review Latin Grammar covers thoroughly and systematically in twenty lessons the necessary syntactical material of the first and second years.

DRILL MATERIAL: A copious amount of drill material (approximately 700 English sentences) provides ample practice in fixing the grammatical principles firmly in the student's mind. Many of these sentences are short enough for oral use. An attempt has been made to include a number of interesting and occasionally amusing sentences in each lesson. A group of passages in connected English prose provides adequate material for reviewing the entire book.

EXPLANATIONS: Care has been taken to make all grammatical explanations concise. Exceptions have been cut to a minimum. In the interest of greater clarity of explanation many of the rules have been printed in diagram form.

WORD CONTENT: The vocabulary used in the exercises is in general that recommended by the College Entrance Examination Board for the first two years.

Review Latin Grammar has been used over the past fifteen years in many public and private schools as well as in a large number of colleges. The present edition of the book is the result of alterations and improvements made in four previous revisions.

A distinguished Latin teacher has recently commended Review Latin Grammar in the following statement:

"The academic soundness of the book and its simplicity of approach allows the teacher to use his own particular method of presentation. I am using Review Latin Grammar in Latin II, III, and IV."

J. K. C.

Andover, Massachusetts
1971

CONTENTS

Lesson   *Page*

   I.   Predicate Nominative. Questions. Relative
       Pronoun. Apposition. The Vocative   1

  II.   The Genitive Case   3

  III.   The Dative (Part 1)   5

  IV.   The Dative (Part 2)   7

  V.   Personal Pronouns. Possessive Adjectives.
       Reflexives 10

  VI.   Ablative with Prepositions. Place Constructions.
       Locative 12

  VII.   Ablative without Prepositions 15

  VIII.   Commands 18

  IX.   Participles 20

  X.   Participles (Including the Ablative Absolute) 22

  XI.   Infinitives (Complementary and Subjective) 25

  XII.   Infinitives in Indirect Statements 27

  XIII.   The Subjunctive: Sequence of Tenses. Purpose.
       Result. Clauses after Verbs of Fearing. 29

  XIV.   Indirect Commands. Substantive Result Clauses . . . 32

  XV.   Indirect Questions. Subordinate Clauses in
       Indirect Statements. 34

  XVI.   Cum Clauses 37

  XVII.   The Gerund and Gerundive 39

  XVIII.   The Passive Periphrastic. 42

  XIX.   Conditional Sentences, Simple and Future 44

  XX.   Conditional Sentences, Contrary to Fact. 46

Connected Prose 48

Vocabulary 51

LESSON I

Predicate Nominative. Questions. The Relative Pronoun. Apposition. The Vocative.

1. Passive verbs take a predicate nominative.
   This includes *fiō*, be made, be done, become, happen.
   > He became king.
   > Rēx factus est.
2. *Inform of* = *certiōrem facere dē* + *abl.* (Make *certior* agree with person informed.)
   > We informed Caesar of the battle.
   > Caesarem certiōrem dē proeliō fēcimus.
   > Caesar was informed of the battle.
   > Caesar certior dē proeliō factus est.
3. *Questions* are introduced by:
   (a) An interrogative word.
   > quis, quid, who, what (pronoun)
   > quī, quae, quod, which, what (adjective)
   > uter-tra-trum, which (of 2)
   > cūr, why
   > ubi, where (in what place)
   > quō, where (to what place)
   (b) -ne appended to first word of sentence (usually the verb)
   (c) Nōnne, expects answer "yes."
   (d) Num, expects answer "no."
4. *The Relative Pronoun*, quī, quae, quod, who, which, agrees with its antecedent in *gender, number,* and *person*. Its *case* depends on its use in its own clause.
   > The girls whom we saw were not beautiful.
   > Puellae quās vīdimus nōn erant pulchrae.
   NOTE: *whose* indicates a *genitive* in Latin: cuius, quōrum, or quārum.
   Be sure to express both the *antecedent* and the *relative* in Latin.
5. An *Appositive* agrees in *case* with the word to which it refers.
   > The Romans, a very brave race, Rōmānī, gēns fortissima.

1

6. The *Vocative* case is used in addressing someone. It is like the *Nominative*, except:

    (a) Second declension nouns and adjectives in *-us* have a vocative singular in *-e*.

        Bonus Brūtus, voc. Bone Brūte.

    (b) Second declension nouns in *-ius* have a vocative singular in *-ī*.

        Fīlius, voc. Fīlī.

    (c) The vocative singular of *meus*-a-um is *mī*, mea, meum.

    NOTE: The vocative is not usually the first word of a sentence.

7.   1. We gave the money to Marcus, a footsoldier.
     2. I shall inform him of the time and place.
     3. What town was burned?
     4. Brutus will be made king.
     5. Has he lost the money which he was carrying?
     6. The queen was informed of the booty which had been captured.
     7. The Rhone, a very beautiful river, is in France.
     8. Who is closing the gates?
     9. We saw many women whose sons had become sailors.
   10. Those mountains are high, are they not?
   11. I gave the letter to a scout who was in camp.
   12. What reward did he give?
   13. Where is the camp, good farmer?
   14. Did you see her today, Marcus?
   15. They found many swords in the towns which they had captured.
   16. Which hand (of the two) do you choose, Anna?
   17. The arrows, a gift of the king, delighted Marcus.
   18. The bridge they built is beautiful.
   19. You did not receive the money (did you), lieutenant?
   20. Where are they going?
   21. What did you say, my son?
   22. They have set fire to the bridge on which we are fighting.
   23. Whose sword have you, Cassius?
   24. Which legion is in camp?
   25. The king will be informed of the book which we sent.
   26. What did you find, boys?
   27. The scouts informed me of the disaster.

28. The farmer to whom I gave the money became my friend.

29. Don't you see the moon, girls?

30. The horseman whose horse had been wounded, fell into a ditch.

NOTE: Sentence 19, do not use *nōn*.

LESSON II

The Genitive Case

8. *The Genitive* has the general meanings: *of*, *'s* (gen. sing.), *s'* (gen. pl).

9. *The Partitive Genitive*

   Part of the men, Pars virōrum

   Note the following words used idiomatically with a Partitive Genitive:

   Plūs, more. More grain (More of grain), Plūs frūmentī

   Satis, enough. Enough men (Enough of men), Satis virōrum

   Nihil, nothing, no. No wine (Nothing of wine), Nihil vīnī

   Aliquid   something, some. Something good (Something of good), anything, any. Aliquid bonī

10. *The Mīlle construction*

    (a) Mīlle, one thousand, is an indeclinable adjective.

        A thousand men, Mīlle virī

    (b) Mīlia, thousands, is a neuter noun followed by the Partitive Genitive. Milia must be used for any number of thousands above 1000.

        Ten thousand men (Ten thousands of men), Decem mīlia virōrum

11. With the following words the partitive idea is expressed by *ex* or *dē* + *ablative*:

    Paucī-ae-a, a few (of)

    Quidam, Quaedam, Quoddam, certain (of)

    Cardinal numbers (of) (For mīlle construction see par. 10)

        A few of the men, Paucī de virīs

        Ten of the soldiers, Decem ex mīlitibus

    NOTE: If there is no partitive idea, the above words are used as agreeing adjectives.

        A few men, Paucī virī

        Certain girls, Quaedam puellae

3

12. The following are agreeing adjectives. They are *not* followed by a genitive.

Omnis-e, all, all of

Reliquus-a-um, rest of

Summus-a-um, top of

Medius-a-um, middle of

Extrēmus-a-um, end of

On top of the hill, In summō colle

13. *The Genitive of Description* must have an agreeing adjective.

noun with A man of great bravery, Vir magnae virtūtis

agreeing adj. (But: A man of bravery = A brave man, Vir fortis)

used to describe A man of this kind, Vir eius modī (*or* huius modī)

inherent A ten foot wall = A wall of ten feet, Mūrus decem pedum

qualities and

measure. *genitive - measure* *ablative - description*

14.
1. All of the citizens
2. Many of the cavalrymen
3. Many states
4. Twelve miles
5. A few of our men
6. A three foot ditch
7. Enough legions
8. The merchants' money
9. Have you any food, slave?
10. A mile
11. Certain of the tribes
12. Two of the girls
13. A few boys
14. A large part of the city
15. All of the hills
16. A two day journey
17. No delay
18. From the middle of the sea
19. A brave soldier
20. Something bad
21. More food
22. All of the money
23. Few of the laws. Few laws
24. Two thousand towns
25. Many of the hostages
26. Certain of the scouts
27. A thousand books
28. A river of great depth
29. He praised a part of the soldiers.
30. States of this kind
31. The rest of the citizens
32. On the top of the rampart
33. At midnight
34. Four of the animals
35. The end of the ditch
36. A twenty foot tower
37. More arms
38. All of the wives
39. Certain of the buildings
40. A very high hill (2 ways)
41. Few of the shields
42. Citizens of this kind
43. Into the middle of the ditch
44. All the rivers
45. Three of the javelins. Three javelins

LESSON III

The Dative (Part I)

[handwritten: shows that some person has some interest in the action of the verb]

15.

┌───┐
| TO + NOUN (or PRONOUN) |
├───┤

Dative of Indirect Object with verbs meaning: give, show, tell, entrust, etc.

He gave money to the queen.
(He gave the queen money.)
Rēgīnae pecūniam dedit.

───

Ad + Accusative with verbs of motion over space: go, run, arrive (at), call or summon (someone) to, hasten (contendō or properō)

He went to town.
Ad oppidum iit.

└───┘

NOTE: *Mātūrō*, Hasten, must be accompanied by an infinitive.

16. *Dative of Possessor*
   He has a horse. A horse is to him.
   Equus est ei.
(This sentence may also be written: Equum habet.)

17. *Dative of Purpose* ~ 6
   He chose a place for a camp.
   Locum castris dēlēgit.

18. *Double Dative* composed of a *Dative of Purpose* and a *Dative of Reference*.
   He was a great help to us.
   Erat magnō auxiliō nōbīs.
          Purpose   Reference

auxiliō, help, aid, advantage, advantageous
praesidiō, guard, protection
subsidiō, reinforcement
ūsuī, use, advantage, advantageous, useful
impedimentō, hindrance
cūrae, care

19. *Dative after Adjectives* meaning: *near*, also, *fit, friendly, pleasing, like*, and their opposites.

> The camp is near the river.
> Castra sunt propīnqua flūminī.
> The town is like a fort.
> Oppidum est simile castellō.

NOTE: The following adjectives are followed by a *genitive*:
similis, like, when followed by a *noun referring to a person* or by a *personal pronoun* (meī, tuī, etc.)
perītus, skilled in, and *imperītus*, unskilled in
avidus ⎫
cupidus⎬ eager for, desirous of

> He is not like me.
> Nōn est similis meī.
> He was skilled in war.
> Erat perītus bellī.
> All men are eager for peace.
> Omnēs sunt avidī pācis.

20. 1. Money is useful to us.
2. He gave Caesar two of the buildings.
3. Brutus has three swords.
4. Will they go to the sea?
5. The wall is near the street.
6. Is he like you, Marcus?
7. They are unskilled in these things.
8. I shall send a letter to father.
9. The swamp was a great hindrance to our men.
10. The cavalry arrived at the village.
11. Our lieutenant was given a reward.
12. The whole city was like a camp.
13. They told Brutus the cause of the war.

6

14. Gifts are pleasing to little boys.
15. He had ten children. (2 ways)
16. My son is not like me.
17. A high rampart is an advantage to the soldiers.
18. They ran to the high hills.
19. He had formed a plan for the journey.
20. Women are never eager for war.
21. We shall come to Long Island.
22. They hastened to the swamp.
23. Is she unfriendly to you, son?
24. He hastened to inform me of the reward.
25. I called all the scouts to me.
26. The departure of the Germans was like flight.
27. Three thousand men were sent to reinforce (as a reinforcement to) these cohorts.
28. I told him something new.
29. Horses have four feet. (2 ways)
30. Children are a great care.
31. We shall arrive at camp today.
32. She was like mother.
33. He is skilled in weapons of this kind.

LESSON IV

The Dative (Part II)

21. *Dative with Compounded Verbs.* Some verbs compounded with *ad, ante, con, dē, in, inter, ob, post, prae, prō, sub,* and *super* are *intransitive* and are used with the Dative.

He is in command of the army.

Exercitui praeest.

(a) Certain compounded verbs are *transitive* and have an Accusative direct object as well as a Dative.

He put Brutus in command of the army.

Brūtum exercituī praefēcit.

(b) Some common compounded verbs used with the Dative are:

Appropīnquō, approach

Dēsum, fail

Bellum īnferō, make war on

Occurrō, meet, run to meet

Praecipiō, instruct

Praeficiō, put (acc.) in command of (dat.)

Praesum, be in command of, be in charge of

22. *Dative with Special Verbs*

Believe	crēdō-ere, crēdidi, crēditum
Favor	faveō-ēre, favī, fautum
Please	placeō-ēre, placuī, placitum
Trust	cōnfidō-ere, cōnfisus sum
Command	imperō, 1
Obey	pareō-ēre, paruī, paritūrus
Pardon	ignōscō-ere, ignōvī, ignōtum
Persuade	persuādeō-ēre, persuāsī, persuāsum
Resist	resistō-ere, restitī, ———
Serve	serviō-īre, servīvī (serviī) servītum
Spare	parcō-ere, peperci, parsūrus
Harm	noceō-ēre, nocui, nocitūrus
Envy	invideō-ēre, invidi, ———
Threaten	minor-ārī, minātus sum

23. *Intransitive Verbs in the Passive* must be used *impersonally*. The Dative is kept.

(Active) Caesar persuaded them.

Caesar eīs persuāsit.

(Passive) They were persuaded by Caesar.

(It was persuaded to them by Caesar.)

Eīs ā Caesare persuāsum est.

(Notice that *persuāsum* is *Neuter*, and that impersonal *it* is not expressed in Latin.)

NOTE: Transitive compounded verbs used with the Dative (Cf. par. 21(a)) are used *personally* in the passive.

Brutus was put in command of the army.

Brūtus exercituī praefectus est.

8

24. 1. I do not trust you, Cassius.
    2. We made war on the Germans.
    3. Who is in command of the fleet?
    4. Shall we spare those hostages?
    5. The captives will be pardoned.
    6. Heavy arms are a hindrance to a footsoldier.
    7. He obtained a new sword.
    8. They do not dare to resist us.
    9. He hastened to the chief.
    10. He hastened to complete the work.
    11. Nobody was harmed.
    12. That bridge is a great advantage to them.
    13. A brave man will be put in command of our legion.
    14. What did he say to the soldiers?
    15. Few of those girls please him.
    16. They have crushed the enemy, men.
    17. They bring in no wine.
    18. Labienus will be in command of the tenth legion.
    19. Disaster threatens the smaller states.
    20. That house is near the forest.
    21. I shall meet father.
    22. A new book will be given as a reward.
    23. Will you not obey me, son?
    24. The safety of the soldiers is a care to the general.
    25. I shall not harm you, slave.
    26. The consul is in charge of the first legion.
    27. Did they meet the enemy's cavalry?
    28. Delay is advantageous to the Germans.
    29. They were approaching the territory of the Helvetians.
    30. He serves a good master.
    31. The river was a help to us.
    32. Food failed the wretched inhabitants.
    33. These Germans were not persuaded.
    34. Do they surpass us?
    35. Who has been in command of our army?
    36. Will they dare to make war on us?

Personal Pronouns. Possessive Adjectives. Reflexives.

25.		PERSONAL PRONOUNS		POSSESSIVE ADJECTIVES
1	ego, I mei, of me mihi mē mē		nōs, we nostrum (nostri), of us nōbis nōs nōbis	meus-a-um, my, mine noster-tra-trum, our, ours
2	tū, you tui, of you tibi tē tē		vōs, you vestrum (vestri), of you vōbis vōs vōbis	tuus-a-um, your, yours vester-tra-trum, your, yours
3	Reflexive	sui sibi sē (sēsē) sē (sēsē)	} him (self) her (self) them (selves)	suus-a-um, his (own), her (own), their (own)
	Non-Reflex.	Forms of *is, ea, id*, him, her, it, them		(*eius*, his, her) (*eōrum, eārum*, their)

NOTE: *Nostrum*, of us, and *Vestrum*, of you, are used as Partitive Genitives.

   Part of us, Pars nostrum

The alternate forms, *Nostri* and *Vestri*, are used objectively.

   Love of (for) you, Amor vestri

26. *TEST FOR REFLEXIVES*: REFLEXIVES MUST (1) STAND IN THE PREDICATE OF THE ENGLISH SENTENCE, *AND* (2) REFER BACK TO THE SUBJECT THROUGH THE VERB.

He loves himself.	We saw his friends.
Sē amat.	Eius amicōs vidimus.
He loves his country.	Their friends have come.
Suam patriam amat.	Eōrum amici vēnērunt.

NOTE: Ipse, self, is *not* usually a reflexive.

He himself said it.   He said it himself.

Ipse id dīxit.   Ipse id dīxit.

27. The preposition *cum* is attached to the end of certain of the personal pronouns in the Ablative case: Mēcum, Tēcum, Sēcum, Nōbīscum, Vōbīscum (also Quibuscum).

28.
1. He intrusted himself to us.
2. He will draw up his line of battle.
3. He went to town with her.
4. They praise us, but we do not praise them.
5. Will you go with me, my friend?
6. The girls fled to their father.
7. We saw the general and his legions.
8. Will you come into my province, Caesar?
9. Fathers ought to trust their sons.
10. His friends are awaiting our arrival.
11. Have they heard our shouts?
12. They fortified the camp themselves.
13. Has he found his sword?
14. We saw a part of you, soldiers.
15. We praise your love for us (of us), Brutus.
16. He was informed of their plan.
17. You will return to your work, soldiers.
18. Caesar and his men have fortified our camp.
19. He has given their books to us.
20. He repaired the ship himself.
21. The legion which he has with him is very brave.
22. We shall put Brutus himself in charge of this cohort.
23. The men with whom we set out have gone away.
24. The merchants carried their money with them.
25. We shall return to their city.
26. His army is a great advantage to you, Caesar.
27. He ordered his men to give the booty to him.
28. I shall not leave you, my brave friends.
29. He has called two thousand soldiers to him.
30. We wounded a few of them.

31. He loves himself, but we do not love him.

32. Our tribe is unlike yours, Antonius.

33. You cannot see yourselves.

34. Boys, have you seen my animals in your father's forest?

35. Certain of his soldiers have betaken themselves to the rear.

36. His legion was being praised by all the citizens.

37. I made it myself.

38. Did he carry enough water with him?

39. Our daughter's friend likes himself.

40. Their javelins are long, but their swords are short.

LESSON VI

Ablative with Prepositions. Place Constructions. Locative.

29. *Prepositions used with the Ablative*: sub, under, at the foot of; *prae*, before, at the head of, compared with; *sine*, without; *ab* (*ā*), by, from; *dē*, down from, concerning; *ex* (*ē*), out of; *prō*, before, for, in behalf of; *cum*, with; *in*, in, on.

    (a) Before *vowels and h*, *ab* and *ex* are used; *before consonants* either *ā* or *ab*; *ē* or *ex*.

    (b) *in* meaning *into*, *against*, is used with the Accusative.

    (c) *sub* meaning *to a position under*, is used with the Accusative.

30. *In with the Ablative* is used *only* in Place Where. (See paragraph 33)

31. *Cum with the Ablative*

    (a) *Accompaniment* (along with)

He came with father.	He fought with (against) with Germans.
Cum patre vēnit.	Cum Germānīs pugnāvit.

    (b) *Manner* (often equal to an English adverb) must have *cum* or an agreeing adjective, or both *cum* and an adjective.

    With great care, Magnā (cum) cūrā

32. *Ab* (*ā*) *with the Ablative*

    (a) *Personal Agent* with a Passive Verb

    He was sent by the king.

    Ab rēge missus est.

(b) *Separation*

He kept the sailors from the island.

Nautās ab īnsulā prohibuit.

NOTE: *Ab* (*ā*) is omitted with *careō*, lack, and is usually omitted with *līberō*, free from, and *prīvō*, deprive of.

They lack money.

Pecūniā carent.

(c) *Place from which* (See diagram below)

33. *Summary of Place Constructions:*

	Regular	With *Names of Cities, Towns, Domus,* home, and *Rūs,* country (opposite of city), ALL PREPOSITIONS ARE OMITTED.
Place From	*Ab, Ex, Dē* + *Ablative* from the city, ab urbe down from the hill, de colle out of the city, ex urbe	*Ablative* from Rome, Rōmā from home, domō; from the country, rūre
Place To	*Ad or In* + *Accusative* to the city, ad urbem into the city, in urbem	*Accusative* to Rome, Rōmam (to) home, domum to the country, rūs
Place Where	*In* + *Ablative* in the city, in urbe on the sea, in marī	*LOCATIVE* at (in) Rome, Rōmae at home, domī in the country, rūrī
		Locative Endings: *Sing. Pl.* I -ae -īs II -ī -īs III -ī(e) -ibus

NOTE: With *urbs* and *oppidum* the preposition is used, and the name of the town is in apposition with the form of urbs or oppidum.

In the city of Rome, In urbe Rōmā

34. Place Names for use with the following exercises:

Cities and Towns	Countries
Carthage, Carthāgō-inis, f.	Belgium, Belgium-ī, n.
Corinth, Corinthus-ī, f.	Italy, Ītalia-ae, f.
Florence, Flōrentia-ae, f.	
Newton, Noviodonum-ī, n.	
Syracuse, Syrācūsae-ārum, f.	Continent
Veii, Vēii-ōrum, m.	Europe, Eurōpa-ae, f.

A

1. In our town
2. At home
3. To Florence
4. In Newton
5. To Italy
6. In the country (opposite of city)
7. In the city of Syracuse
8. To Corinth
9. Into the city
10. From Carthage
11. In Europe
12. To Veii
13. From the country (opposite of city)
14. In Carthage
15. From Belgium
16. To Europe
17. In the town of Veii
18. To Carthage
19. From home
20. From the city of Florence
21. In this country
22. In Corinth
23. From Italy
24. In Syracuse

B

1. He ran with great speed.
2. They struggled with the enemy.
3. We wounded him with spears.
4. He lacks wine and food.
5. Shall I go home with you, Anna?
6. He came from Italy.
7. They had deprived us of our freedom.
8. Shall I depart without them?
9. He is staying at the foot of the mountain.
10. Are your friends in town, Marcus?
11. My wife has gone to the country.
12. Many things were done by slaves.

13. Is he in the city of Corinth?

14. The boys who came from Carthage lacked speed.

15. He was freed from all fear.

16. They surpass us in number of men.

17. You ought to work zealously, boys.

18. They cannot keep us from the wall.

19. Those javelins were thrown with great force.

20. War deprived the wretched inhabitants of food.

21. There are many thousand men on the hill.

22. They were defeated by the bravery of our infantry.

23. Many wars have been waged with the Germans.

24. He killed the animal with a stone.

25. Brave men fight bravely for (pro) their country (native land).

LESSON VII

The Ablative Without Prepositions

35. *Ablative of Means*

      He fought with a sword.   Gladiō pugnābat.

  (a) Five Deponents are used with the Ablative of Means; *Ūtor*, use; *Fruor*, enjoy; *Fungor*, perform; *Potior*, get possession of; *Vescor*, feed on.

36. *Ablative of Cause*

They suffer from fear.	I am delighted at your return.
Timōre labōrant.	Reditū tuō dēlector.

  (a) Prepositions are used in a few expressions like: *Quā dē causā*, for this reason; *Quā ex rē*, for this reason.

37. *Ablative of Time When or Within Which*

      In the winter, Hieme. Within three hours, Tribus hōris.

Notice the difference between the *Ablative of Time When* and the *Accusative of Extent of Time.*

      He worked during the night (tells when).

      Nocte labōrābat.

      He worked for three hours (tells how long).

      Trēs hōrās labōrābat.

38. *Ablative of Specification*

They surpass us in speed.

Nōs celeritāte superant.

(a) *Dignus*, worthy (of) and *Indignus*, unworthy (of), are used with an Ablative of Specification.

(b) *Maior nātū*, older; *Minor nātū*, younger

39. *Ablative of Description* (*Must* have an agreeing adjective.)

A man of great courage, Vir magnā virtūte

NOTE: The Genitive of Description (Cf. par. 13), *magnae virtūtis*, would have the same meaning. (With *eius modī* and *huius modī*, of this kind, the genitive is required.)

40. *Ablative of Comparison*

After a comparative, *than* is expressed in one of the following ways:

(a) *Quam*. (The 2 persons or things compared are usually the same case.)

Marcus is taller than Anna.

Mārcus est altior quam Anna.

(b) *Ablative of Comparison without Quam*. (This construction is used only when 2 Nominatives or 2 Accusatives are compared; otherwise Quam is used.)

Marcus is taller than Anna.

Mārcus est altior Annā.

But: Marcus' head is larger than Anna's.

Mārcī caput est maius quam Annae.

NOTE: With *Plūs*, more (than), *Minus*, less (than), *Amplius*, more (than), and *Longius*, longer (than), *Quam* may be omitted without changing the case of the second person or thing compared.

He saw less than three sailors.

Minus trēs nautās vīdit.

41. *Ablative of Degree of Difference*

Marcus is a foot taller (taller by a foot) than Anna.

Mārcus est pede altior quam Anna.

NOTE: Paulō, a little (by a little); Multō, much (by much)

42. 1. They will return within two months.
   2. He is faster than the wind.
   3. They were terrified by the sudden attack.
   4. I fled with the rest of the soldiers.
   5. He persuaded us by the speech.

16

6. She is more friendly to me than to you, Marcus.
7. Nights are much shorter in the summer.
8. They suffered from lack of water.
9. We worked for more than four hours.
10. Is he older than my brother?
11. For this reason we deprived the Germans of weapons.
12. Did he use the ships?
13. This river is wider than that.
14. There were many wounds on his body.
15. Caesar was a man of great influence.
16. He could not see the river on account of the trees.
17. Villages are much smaller than cities.
18. The enemy were defeated by the courage of our infantry.
19. The Germans enjoy war.
20. He defended himself with a shield.
21. He set out at daybreak.
22. This boy is small because he is rather young.
23. The consuls were men of courage.
24. That building is much higher than the wall.
25. The valley was filled with water.
26. A storm delayed me for five days.
27. My foot is a little larger than my hand.
28. This lieutenant is unworthy of gratitude.
29. Many legions remained in winter quarters in the winter.
30. Will you complete the work carefully, Antonius?
31. A Roman general, Caesar by name, got possession of that region.
32. He was easily persuaded (Cf. par. 23) by money.
33. Next year he will build not less than three bridges.
34. For this reason our shouts were not heard by the scouts.
35. He sailed from Veii to Syracuse.
36. In that land there is a beautiful city, Florence by name.
37. All men enjoy good food.
38. Caesar's ships were larger than the Britons'.
39. I saw a broader river than the Rhone.
40. This route is more difficult for the infantry than for the cavalry.

LESSON VIII

Commands

43. *An Imperative* expresses an order. Imperatives are in the second person.

Active Verbs		Deponents	
Singular	*Plural*	*Singular*	*Plural*
I Pugnā	Pugnāte	Hortāre	Hortāminī
II Monē	Monēte	Verēre	Verēminī
III Pōne	Pōnite	Sequere	Sequiminī
Cape	Capite	Ēgredere	Ēgrediminī
IV Audī	Audīte	Potīre	Potīminī

Warn them, Marcus.   Follow me, Marcus.
Monē eōs, Mārce.   Sequere mē, Mārce.
Hear this, men.   Go out, soldiers.
Audīte hoc, virī.   Ēgrediminī, mīlitēs.

(a) *Dico, Duco, Facio,* and *Fero* have the following imperatives:
  Dīc — Dīcite   Fac — Facite
  Dūc — Dūcite   Fer — Ferte

NOTE: All compounds of these verbs (except -ficio compounds) are similarly irregular. Redūc, Īnfer, but Refice

(b) *Scio,* know, and *Memini,* remember, use the future imperative only.
  Scītō — Scītōte   Mementō — Mementōte

(c) *Do not* is expressed by the imperatives *Nōlī* (singular) and *Nōlīte* (plural) followed by a *Present Infinitive.*
  Do not go.   Do not follow.
  Nōlī īre (Nōlīte īre)   Nōlī sequī (Nōlīte sequī)

44. *The Hortatory Subjunctive* (1st or 3rd person, singular and plural) is used in the present tense only. The negative is *nē*.
  Let us go.   Let us not go.   Let it stand.
  Eāmus.   Nē eāmus.   Stet.

18

45. Summary of Commands:

AFFIRMATIVE

Singular	Plural
Laudem, Let me praise.	Laudēmus. Let us praise.
Laudā, Praise.	Laudāte. Praise.
Laudet, Let him praise.	Laudent. Let them praise.

NEGATIVE

Nē laudem. Let me not praise.	Nē laudēmus. Let us not praise.
Nōlī laudāre. Do not praise.	Nōlīte laudāre. Do not praise.
Nē laudet. Let him not praise.	Nē laudent. Let them not praise.

46.
1. Come here, Marcus. Do not go away.
2. Follow the leader, men.
3. Let us not choose him.
4. Use your weapons, Antonius.
5. Do not stay here, soldiers.
6. Let's burn the bridge as soon as possible.
7. Remember this, boys.
8. Do not fall into the ditch, Anna.
9. Believe me, my son.
10. Let us hasten to the fort.
11. Wound him again, Cassius.
12. Do not bring your books, lieutenant.
13. Let him say this, if he wishes.
14. Tell us your story, scout.
15. Lead back the troops, Brutus.
16. Listen, Marcus, do not do that.
17. Let us pray.
18. Hand over the money, farmer.
19. Let us not fear that which we cannot see.
20. Put your feet into the water, girls.
21. Pray for (prō) us.
22. Come quickly, my friends.
23. Do not tell this to the consul, Marcus.
24. Let us not promise him money.
25. Lead out the whole army, general.
26. Let them try to persaude me.

27. Encourage your men, Caesar.

28. Give us enough food, Mother.

29. Let us make war on the Germans.

30. Collect your arms, men.

31. Let us return home.

32. Bring back my bonny (pretty girl) to me.

33. Let us praise brave men.

34. Defend yourselves carefully with your shields.

35. Let us not put Brutus in command of our legion.

36. Make war on our enemies, consul.

LESSON IX

Participles

47. Regular transitive verbs have three participles. In the following diagram the *literal meaning* is given for each participle.

	Active	Passive
Present	Mittēns, (while) sending	
Perfect		Missus-a-um (*having been*) *sent*
Future	Missūrus-a-um, about to send	

48. Deponents have three participles, *all active in meaning*:

Hortāns, (while) urging   Hortātus, *having urged*

Hortātūrus, about to urge

49. The Present Participle denotes action *at same time as*   } the action

    The Perfect Participle denotes action *completed before*   } of the verb

    The Future Participle denotes action *future with reference to* } of its clause

      I found him working.

      Eum *labōrantem* repperī. (Same time)

      The Germans having been captured were killed.

      Germānī *captī* necātī sunt. (Completed)

      We about to die salute you.

      Moritūrī tē salūtāmus. (Future)

50. Participle phrases are often used in Latin for English subordinate clauses: *Temporal* (when, while, after), *Causal* (since, because), *Concessive* (although), *Conditional* (if), *Relative* (who, which), or *Coordinate* (and). Procedure:

Step I — Convert subordinate clause into its corresponding *literal meaning* as a participle.

Step II — Determine case of word with which participle agrees. (Remember that participles have no subjects.)

Step III — Write sentence in Latin, making participle agree in gender, number, and case with the proper word.

Example: *He found the money which had been lost.*

Step I — Having been lost

Step II — *Money* is accusative (object of *found*).

Step III — Pecūniam amissam repperit.

51. The *perfect participles* of some *deponents* are used in practically the sense of English present participles: *Arbitrātus*, thinking; *Ausus*, daring; *Veritus*, fearing.

52. A personal pronoun standing in the main clause and referring to the noun of the participle phrase *is not expressed* in Latin.

Having led out the troops he drew *them* up.

Cōpiās ēductās īnstrūxit.

53. 1. Men who have been killed do not tell stories.

2. He was killed while fighting for his country.

3. After encouraging (cohortor) the men, he departed.

4. I found her writing a letter.

5. Setting out from Rome they marched into Gaul.

6. We were worn out by the war and desired to make peace.

7. When Caesar had been informed of the disaster, he hastened to Rome

8. We met (occurrō) them as they were about to go out.

9. Not daring to reply, I said nothing.

10. Having seized the town, he burned it.

11. The enemy harassed us as we crossed the river.

12. The food sent to our camp was a great help to us.

13. Although the gates have been closed, they will soon be opened.

14. Fearing (vereor) an ambush he did not dare to approach nearer.

15. As he was about to seize me he suddenly fell.

16. If the camp is defended bravely it will not be captured.

17. Have you seen Lost River, Marcus?
18. I do not trust him when he says this.
19. After capturing these soldiers, he sent them to Caesar.
20. Having advanced (progredior) three miles, he pitched camp on the bank of a certain river.
21. We made an attack on the enemy who were approaching.
22. Few of those who had been seen escaped.
23. Fearing (vereor) a storm, he stayed at home.
24. Although we were defeated and driven back into the town, we were not killed.
25. Rewards will be given to the men who have been besieged in that fort.
26. After writing the letter, he sent it to his father.
27. We followed the enemy for seven days and finally lost the road.
28. I saw him returning (redeō) to Italy with you.
29. The ships could not proceed very quickly because they were hindered by storms.
30. Our soldiers, trained by many battles, routed the enemy as they advanced to our fortifications.

NOTE: In sentences 11 and 28 remember that *eo* and its compounds have an irregular present participle: *iēns, euntis*.

LESSON X

Participles (Including the Ablative Absolute)

54. Use the Ablative Absolute construction only when the word with which the participle agrees is *not connected grammatically* (as subject, object, etc.) with the main verb of the sentence. (Remember that *participles do not have subjects.*)

> *Having received the money, he bought the house.*
> Step I — *having been received*
> Step II — *money* (not connected grammatically with *bought*)
> Step III — Pecūniā acceptā, domum ēmit.

(a) In general avoid using a reflexive or an Ablative of Personal Agent within an Ablative Absolute.

When Caesar had done this, he departed.

Hōc factō, Caesar discessit.

(b) Perfect participles of *deponents* normally *agree with the subject of the main verb*. Therefore they are *not* commonly used in the Ablative Absolute.

Having encouraged the men, he began battle.

Step I — *having encouraged*

Step II — *he* is the subject of main verb *began.*

Step III — Virōs cohortātus, proelium commīsit.

55. A Present Participle in an Ablative Absolute has the literal meaning:
With ——ing.

With everybody shouting
Since everybody was shouting } he could not be heard.
While everybody was shouting

Omnibus clāmantibus audīri nōn poterat.

56. The Latin verb *sum* has no present participle. Hence two or more nouns or pronouns (with or without adjectives) may form an Ablative Absolute where the present participle of *sum* (being) should be understood. Learn the following expressions and their English meanings:

Mē cōnsule, In my consulship (lit. I being consul)

Crassō et Pompēiō cōnsulibus, In the consulship of Crassus and Pompey

Caesare duce, Under Caesar's leadership (lit. Caesar being leader)

Mē invītō, Against my will (lit. I being unwilling)

57. 1. Since the work was finished, he went home.
2. Upon learning these things he demanded all the booty.
3. Under the leadership of Marcus we crushed the enemy's horsemen.
4. Having found the soldiers, we led them to camp.
5. Leaving part of the money at home, we started for town.
6. Did you find a few boys working diligently, Brutus?
7. Setting out at midnight, he reached the mountain at daybreak.
8. Although we had driven the men out of the city, we spared the women and children.
9. Not daring to delay longer, they hastened to the woods.
10. While the Germans were besieging the city, we did not have enough food.

11. After encouraging (*cohortor* and *cōnfīrmō*) the soldiers by a short speech, he gave the signal for battle.
12. Nobody saw me when I crossed the swamp.
13. On leaving (*relinquō*) the village we crossed a wide field.
14. Although the children had been snatched from the falling building, we could not find them.
15. They did not dare to depart against my will.
16. In our consulship all the citizens fought bravely for (*prō*) their country.
17. Although many were fleeing, he remained.
18. With Brutus as general nobody feared the enemy's troops.
19. He caught with his hand all of the weapons thrown by the Gauls.
20. We can very easily defend a place fortified by nature.
21. When he had gained possession (*potior* and *occupō*) of the camp, he set out for the river.
22. Since they have been alarmed by this disaster, they will surrender.
23. In the consulship of Caesar and Bibulus war was waged with the Helvetians.
24. After beaching the ships, we carefully hid our arms under a certain tree.
25. When he tried to escape, we seized him.
26. Now that this has been done, we shall tell you everything (all things).
27. He summoned Labienus and put him in command of the tenth legion.
28. Having devastated (*vāstō* and *populor*) the large cities, the Germans began to harass our towns and villages.
29. Leaving eight ships to guard (as a guard to) the harbor, he ordered (*iubeō*) the rest of the sailors to lift anchor and sail to France.
30. After they had brought together a great multitude of weapons and had chosen suitable leaders, they dismissed the council.
31. They drove the German into the river and killed him with arrows.

LESSON XI

Infinitives (Complementary and Subjective)

58. *THE SUBJECT OF AN INFINITIVE IS IN THE ACCUSATIVE.*
59. *Complementary Infinitives* are used to complete the meaning of other verbs such as:

possum, be able, can

cupiō ⎫
volō ⎭ wish

nōlō, be unwilling, not wish

mālō, prefer

iubeō, order

dēbeō, ought

prohibeō, prevent

audeō, dare

coepī, began

cōnor ⎫
temptō ⎭ try, attempt

videor, seem

cōnstituō, decide

mātūrō, hasten

(a) Marcus wishes to depart.
Mārcus discēdere cupit.

(b) Marcus wishes to be a sailor.
Mārcus nauta esse cupit.

Nauta is a predicate nominative agreeing with *Mārcus.*
(Remember that the verb *sum* connects grammatical equals.)

(c) Marcus wishes his son to be a sailor.
Mārcus suum filium esse nautam cupit.

Filium is subject accusative of the infinitive *esse.* (Cf. par. 58)
Nautam is predicate accusative agreeing with *filium.*
(As in sentence (b), the verb *sum* connects grammatical equals.)

(d) He orders the letter to be sent.
Littērās mitti iubet.
(Why is *litterās* accusative?)

(e) They prevented us from departing.
Nōs discēdere prohibēbant.
(What case is *nōs* and why is it in that case?)

✳ (f) They could have come.
Venīre potuērunt.

You ought to have gone.
Īre dēbuistī.

Notice that *could have* and *ought to have* are expressed by the *perfect indicative* of possum and dēbeō with a *present infinitive.*

60. *Subjective Infinitives* are used as the subjects of other verbs, especially

Objective: I want you to fly
(has its own subject)

25

est, erat, erit, etc. Since the infinitive is a *neuter noun,* a predicate adjective agreeing with the infinitive will be *neuter.*

It is good to work. = To work is good (or Working is good.)
Labōrāre est bon*um.*

(Notice that *it* is not expressed in Latin sentences of this type.)

61.
1. He ought to be a merchant.
2. Do you prefer to be left at home, Marcus?
3. It will be difficult to persuade him.
4. We could not have repaired the ships.
5. I do not wish my sons to be farmers.
6. Beautiful girls ought to be praised.
7. He is said to be working.
8. It is bad to be conquered by the enemy.
9. We shall order the javelins to be thrown.
10. Talking is easy.
11. They had begun to move camp.
12. The ladies could have set out for home.
13. He prevented me from breaking my head.
14. Most nations do not dare to harm Americans.
15. She wished her daughter to be seen by all the young men.
16. It is good to enjoy life.
17. He wished his son to be safe.
18. We ought to inform him of the danger.
19. Deceiving a friend is disgraceful.
20. They will not dare to resist us.
21. He ought not to have done that.
22. I shall prevent them from being captured.
23. Those women seem to be unhappy.
24. It is bad to lack money.
25. He could have been a help to his father.
26. She did not wish the letter to be written.
27. They have decided to remain on top of the mountain.
28. It was very difficult to find the place at night.
29. All our citizens want the laws to be just.
30. Marcus is unwilling to be sent home.
31. Why does he prefer to follow others?
32. Seeing is believing.

LESSON XII

Infinitives in Indirect Statements

62. Simple Indirect Statements are composed of:
    (a) Introducing Verb meaning say, think, know, learn, etc.
    (b) Infinitive with Subject Accusative

    The Present Infinitive denotes action happening
    at same time as ⎫ the action of
    The Perfect Infinitive denotes action happening ⎬ introducing
    before ⎭ verb
    The Future Infinitive denotes action happening
    after

    He says that he is writing.
    Dīcit sē scrībere. (same time)
    He says that he has written (wrote).
    Dīcit sē scrīpsisse. (time before)
    He says that he will write.
    Dīcit sē scrīptūrum (esse). (time after)
    He said that he was writing.
    Dīxit sē scrībere. (same time)
    He said that he had written.
    Dīxit sē scrīpsisse. (time before)
    He said that he would write.
    Dīxit sē scrīptūrum (esse). (time after)

63. Use *Negō*, deny, say —— not, instead of *Dīcō* —— *nōn*.

64. Verbs meaning *promise to, hope to,* and *expect to* are usually followed
    by a *Future Infinitive* with subject accusative.
    He hoped to see her. = He hoped that he would see her.
    Spērāvit sē eam vīsūrum (esse).

65. In place of the rarely used Future Passive Infinitive, use:
    Fore (or *Futūrum esse*) + *Ut* (Ut —— *nōn*) with Subjunctive verb
    (*present subjv.* if introducing verb is present, *imperfect subjv.* if introduc-
    ing verb is past).
    He says that the letter will be written.
    Dīcit fore ut litterae scrībantur.
    He knew that the letter would not be sent.
    Scīvit fore ut litterae nōn mitterentur.

(a) The same construction is used to represent *a missing Future Active Infinitive*.

We think that the legion will halt.

Putāmus fore ut legiō cōnsistat.

(b) But *Possum* uses its *Present Infinitive* in place of the missing Future Inf.

He thought that he would be able to go.

Putāvit sē īre posse.

66. 1. Do you think that he is at home?
   2. He said that many stones had been thrown.
   3. She thinks she is safe.
   4. They reported that the horsemen were being sent ahead.
   5. He promised to return within three years.
   6. We know that the Germans lacked ships.
   7. I hope that you will be able to see the fleet.
   8. He replied that a few of the legions had been sent to Rome.
   9. Do you expect to be in the country next summer, Anna?
   10. We informed him that two thousand men were pitching camp on the shore.
   11. Did he say that the larger part of our army would be defeated?
   12. We expect to increase the number of legions.
   13. He learned that many men were being killed in his country.
   14. I think that I shall demand reinforcements.
   15. He said that he did not fear their conspiracy.
   16. I know she will help you, Tullius.
   17. They write that certain of our cohorts have been routed.
   18. Many men thought that she was very beautiful.
   19. We think that the money will be found soon.
   20. A few nations had already promised to send help.
   21. Did the scouts report that the mountain had been captured?
   22. We saw that it would be rather difficult to expel him.
   23. He hoped that his men had not harmed the women and children.
   24. They announced that the fiercest attacks of the enemy were being withstood.
   25. We hear that he has lost all the money.
   26. The lieutenant reported that he had carried the wounded soldier three miles.

27. I knew that he would not fear (timeō-ēre, timuī, ——) the attack.
28. She expects to see him in Rome.
29. The Germans promised to send cavalry.
30. Did you tell Marcus that the fortifications had been destroyed?
31. We hope that she will trust us.

LESSON XIII

The Subjunctive: Sequence of Tenses. Purpose.
Result. Clauses after Verbs of Fearing.

67. The tense of all dependent subjunctives is regularly determined by the following diagram:

	Introducing Verb	Subjunctive Clause
Primary Sequence	Present Future Fut. Perf.	Present (Incompleted Action) Perfect (Completed Action)
Secondary (History) Sequence	Any Past Tense	Imperfect (Incompleted Action) *aorist perfect* Pluperfect (Completed Action)

always incomplete, never uses inf.

68. *Purpose Clauses*: *Ut*, (in order) that, to. *Nē*, (in order) that —— not.
Subjunctive, Present or Imperfect only (according to diagram par. 67)

He comes (in order) that he may see her.   Venit ut eam videat.
(in order) to see her.

The girl departed (in order) that she might not be seen.
Puella discessit nē vidērētur.

(a) *Relative Clauses of Purpose*: *Quī, Quae, Quod* may replace *Ut* when there is an expressed antecedent.
He sent men (who were) to do this.
Virōs mīsit quī hoc facerent.

(b) When a *comparative* stands in the Purpose Clause, *Quō* may replace *Ut*.
He threw away his sword that he might run more easily.
Gladium abiēcit quō facilius curreret.

69. *Result Clauses*: *Ut*, so that. *Ut* —— *nōn*, so that —— not. Subjunctive, generally Present or Imperfect.

NOTE: *Tam*, so, so very; *Sīc*, so, in such a way; *Ita*, so, so very, in such a way; or *Tantus-a-um*, so large, so great, often precede a Result Clause.

He ran so fast that he could not be caught.
Tam celeriter cucurrit ut capī nōn posset.

(a) Negative Result Clauses and Negative Purpose Clauses differ in their use of introducing words. Study the following:

	Negative Purpose	*Negative Result*
that —— not	nē	ut —— nōn
that —— no one	nē quis	ut —— nēmō
that —— nothing	nē quid	ut —— nihil
that —— never	nē umquam	ut —— numquam

70. *Clauses after Verbs of Fearing*: *Nē*, that, lest. *Ut*, that —— not. Subjunctive, usually Present or Imperfect.

He fears that he may lose the money.
Timet nē pecūniam amittat.
He feared that we would not come.
Veritus est ut venīrēmus.
He feared that the town had been captured.
Timēbat nē oppidum expugnātum esset.

(a) When the verb of fearing means *to be afraid to*, an *infinitive* follows.
He was afraid to go out.
Timēbat exīre.

71. 1. They ran so fast that they were able to surpass all the others.
2. He always waits here to see us.
3. I am afraid that you do not trust me, Cassius.
4. In order not to be seen, he hid himself behind a tree.
5. Are you afraid to return home alone, girls?
6. He was wounded so severely that he remained with us for a long time.
7. So great is his influence that nobody dares to attack him.
8. He will destroy the letter in order that nobody may learn our plans.
9. They had come to inform us of the route.
10. We feared that he would perish from hunger.

30

11. He was never afraid to help a friend.
12. We captured the fort so quickly that the general could not flee.
13. In order to get possession of the other bank more easily, he built a bridge across the river.
14. We have so few men that we are accomplishing nothing.
15. That man will kill himself in order that he may never be captured alive.
16. He is afraid that the cavalry have been routed by the attack.
17. He held us in winter quarters so that we might not be able to report the matter.
18. They sent ahead certain of the soldiers to learn the nature of the region.
19. The enemy are losing so many men that they can be defeated easily.
20. Three thousand farmers assembled to repulse the British.
21. Has he a shield with which to defend himself?
22. So great a silence filled the woods that the voice of the wind could be heard.
23. They feared that a few of the ships had been destroyed by the storm.
24. He found so large a supply of money that he could not carry it.
25. His men chose the swiftest horses in order to overtake us more quickly.
26. What frightens you, Antonius? Are you afraid to meet him?
27. We were afraid that you were not at home, my friend.
28. He was so terrified by the slaughter of the animals that he never wished to see that place again.
29. Will he try to see her in Athens?
30. That river is so deep that nobody can cross it without a boat.
31. She spends the winter in Florida that she may never be sick.
32. Was Marcus afraid that we would surrender all our possessions to the Gauls?
33. He said this in order that the allies might fight more boldly.
34. They feared that we would not send reinforcements.
35. We marched all night in order to reach home as soon as possible.

Indirect Commands. Substantive Result Clauses.

72. *Indirect Commands*

Introducing Verb	Person asked, ordered, etc.	Indirect Command
Ask, *Rogō* All other verbs meaning } Ask, Beg, Demand }	Accusative Ab + Ablative	*Ut*, that, to *Nē*, that —— not, not to
Order (Give an order to) *Imperō* } *Mandō* }	Dative	Negative Indirect Commands, like negative Purpose Clauses, always begin with *Nē*.
Persuade, *Persuādeō*	Dative	(Cf. par. 69 (a))
Urge, *Hortor*	Accusative	
Advise, Warn, *Moneō*	Accusative	Subjunctive, *Present* or *Imperfect only* (Cf. par. 67)
Allow, Permit (Give permission to), *Permittō*	Dative	

He asks me to come.   He persuaded us not to go away.

Mē rogat ut veniam.   Nōbīs persuāsit nē discēderēmus.

NOTE: *Iubeō*, order, and *Patior*, permit, allow, are exceptions and have the Infinitive with Subject Accusative.

He ordered them to go away.   Eōs iussit discēdere.

73. *Substantive Result Clauses*

Introducing Verb	Substantive Result Clause
Cause, Make, Bring it about { *Faciō* *Efficiō* *Perficiō*	*Ut*, that *Ut* —— *nōn*, that —— not (or *Ut* —— *nēmō*; *Ut* —— *nihil*; *Ut* —— *numquam*) (Cf. par. 69 (a))
It happens { *Fit* *Accidit*	
It remains { *Restat* *Reliquum est*	Subjunctive, usually *Present* or *Imperfect*. (Cf. par. 67)
It is the custom, *Mōs est* Added to this is the fact, *Additur*	

It happened that nobody was at home.

Accidit ut nēmō esset domī.

He made everything seem easy. (He brought it about that everything seemed easy.)

Effēcit ut omnia facilia vidērentur.

74.
1. I urged him not to hesitate.
2. It is the custom of women to talk for a long time.
3. He asked (*rogo* and *quaero*) me to go to Syracuse.
4. We advised them to say nothing.
5. It happens that he is doing nothing today.
6. You could have urged (Cf. par. 59 (f)) them not to set out, Marcus.
7. It is good to fight for the native land.
8. He will not allow (*permitto* and *patior*) us to cross the river.
9. I ordered (*impero* and *iubeo*) him to halt.
10. Added to this is the fact that he never complains.
11. It happened that nobody tried to find us.
12. Let us advise her not to buy that swamp.
13. Will he persuade us to undertake this work?
14. He caused us to understand all these things.
15. I warn you, Antonius, not to go through that valley.
16. We asked them to keep still.
17. They brought it about that the hostages were returned alive.
18. Did he persuade the other consul to make war on the Gauls?
19. We shall not allow (*patior* and *permitto*) those merchants to remain here.
20. Caesar ordered (*impero* and *iubeo*) the camp to be fortified.
21. Wars often cause the number of citizens to be lessened.
22. Men, I advise you not to await the arrival of your friends.
23. It is the custom of certain girls to wander through the streets at night.
24. Will you allow this man to be arrested, lieutenant?
25. He ordered (*impero* and *iubeo*) the baggage to be left in that place.
26. This man caused peace to be made with the neighboring tribes.
27. I ask you not to weep, good lady.
28. Will he demand that the hostages be sent soon?
29. He urged us to be brave.
30. The Germans were so terrified that they asked us to spare them.

31. They did not allow the bridge to be built.

32. She ordered (*imperō*) him never to return.

33. And so it happened that he never saw her again.

34. I warned the girl not to believe him.

LESSON XV

Indirect Questions. Subordinate Clauses in Indirect Statements.

75. *Indirect Questions* are introduced by a verb meaning Ask, Learn, Know, Tell, etc. They begin with an *interrogative word* (Who, What, Where, Why). They have their verb in the *Subjunctive*, tense determined by the rule for Sequence in par. 67.

	Introducing Verb	Indirect Question
Primary	I ask, *Rogō* I shall ask, *Rogābō*	what you do, are doing, *quid faciās*. (pr.) what you did, have done, *quid fēceris*. (per.)
Secondary	I asked, *Rogābam* *Rogāvī* I had asked, *Rogāveram*	what you did, were doing *quid facerēs*. (imp.) what you had done, *quid fēcissēs*. (plu.)

(a) Indirect Questions referring to the *future* use the Subjunctive of the *Future Periphrastic* (fut. participle + the pr. or imp. subjunctive of *sum*.)

I ask what you will do.   I asked what you would do.
Rogō quid factūrus sis.   Rogāvī quid factūrus essēs.

(b) Where (*in* what place), *Ubi*
    Where (*to* what place, *Quō*

(c) Whether, *Num*
    Whether ——— or, *Utrum* ——— *an*, -*ne* ——— *an*
    Whether ——— or not, *Utrum* ——— *necne*

(d) Notice how an *Indirect Question* differs from a *Relative Clause*:
    (1) An Indirect Question is introduced by Ask, Learn, Know, etc.
    (2) A Relative has an *Antecedent*; an Interrogative has none.

34

76. *Subordinate Clauses in Indirect Statements* have their verbs in the *Subjunctive*; tense of Subjunctive determined by the Introducing Verb (Say, Think, etc.) according to the rule in par. 67.

> He says that he will find the money which he lost.
> Dīcit sē pecūniam repertūrum esse quam āmīserit.
> He said that he saw the men who were following.
> Dīxit sē vidēre virōs quī sequerentur.

(a) *A Future Perfect Indicative* of a Direct Statement becomes (as a subordinate verb) in an *Indirect Statement*:

> Perfect Subjunctive in Primary Sequence
> Pluperfect Subjunctive in Secondary Sequence
> Direct Statement: "If the book is returned, I will give a reward."
> "Sī liber redditus erit, praemium dabō."

Indirect Statement:

> Dīcit sī liber redditus sit (perf. subj.) sē praemium datūrum esse.
> Dīxit sī liber redditus esset (plu. subj.) sē praemium datūrum esse.

77. 1. I asked him why he was following me.
  2. We shall learn where he has gone.
  3. The merchant thought that he would hide the money which he had made.
  4. They do not wish to tell us in what city they are staying.
  5. Those men informed us that they had come to free the hostages.
  6. He asked with great care what the men had said.
  7. I can easily learn what he found.
  8. Tell us, slave, whether your master is at home.
  9. If we collect (fut. perf.) enough men, the enemy will not attack us.
  10. I know that if we collect enough men, the enemy will not attack us.
  11. I knew that if we collected enough men, the enemy would not attack us.
  12. He asked why this was not being done faster.
  13. I cannot learn whether she has set out or is waiting at home.
  14. We all knew which legion he had sent.
  15. We think that the legion which he has sent ahead will perish in the swamp.
  16. They asked what he would reply.
  17. We heard that he had killed the eagle which was harassing many small animals.

18. She never told him whether she wished to go or not.
19. We hope to find the very stone with which the general was killed.
20. He asked us where the sword had been put.
21. I am trying to learn which hill they will fortify.
22. I thought that he would get possession of the hill which was near camp.
23. He was in the city to which we were being sent.
24. They know to which city we were sent.
25. He had often said that the Germans would be defeated. (Cf. par. 65)
26. I do not know whether he saw me or not.
27. Don't you see that the soldiers whom you summoned are being driven back?
28. He knows what plan he will form.
29. When (cum) the bridge is built (fut. perf.), our men will cross the river.
30. He says that when the bridge is built, our men will cross the river.
31. He said that when the bridge was built, our men would cross the river.
32. Do you know which of the (two) brothers can be persuaded? (Cf. par. 23)
33. They learned from the scouts which town had been burned.
34. Who will tell me what mountain I can see from this place?
35. I shall never do what you have ordered, Cassius.
36. We saw that nothing would be done unless we ourselves helped.
37. I know why he does not dare to use force.
38. He reported that the city was being defended by men who were throwing weapons from the top of the walls.
39. He says he is preventing the ships from being sent because they ought to be repaired.
40. We shall not tell you what we saw that day in the city of Florence.
41. They told us where they would spend the winter.

LESSON XVI

Cum Clauses.

78. *Cum, Since* (Causal) and *Cum, Although* (Concessive) are always used
with the *Subjunctive*, tense determined by the main verb according to
rule in par. 67.

Since he does not dare to fight, he stays in camp.

Cum pugnāre nōn audeat, in castrīs manet.

Although many had set out, few however, returned.

Cum multī profectī essent, paucī tamen revertērunt.

79. *Cum, When* (Temporal)

(a) Referring to *Present* or *Future*, use *Indicative* (Present, Future, or
Fut. Perf.)

When he fights, he wins.

Cum pugnat, vincit.

When I find it, I will return.

Cum id inveniam (or invēnerō), revertar.

NOTE: The Future Perfect is used to indicate that an action is completed
in the future.

(b) Referring to *Past*, use *Subjunctive (Imperfect or Pluperfect only)*.

Cum + Imperfect Subjunctive means *When* or *While*.

When (While) he was fighting, he was killed.

Cum pugnāret, interfectus est.

Cum + Pluperfect Subjunctive means *When* or *After*.

When (After) he had said this, he departed.

Cum hoc dīxisset, abiit.

NOTE: *Cum, When*, is occasionally used with the past tenses of the
Indicative to date or define the time of the action of the main verb. In
this use Cum is often found in the following combinations: *Tum cum*, At
the time when, and *Eō tempore cum*, At the time when.

He received great praise when he said this.

Magnam laudem accēpit cum id dīxit.

At the time when father had lost all the money, I was away.

Eō tempore cum pater omnem pecūniam amīserat, aberam.

80. When an *expressed subject* of a subordinate verb refers to the same person or thing as that of the main verb, place the subject *first*, followed by the subordinate clause.

> While Brutus was returning home, he fell into the river.
> Brūtus cum domum redīret, in flūmen dēcidit.

81.   1. Since our men have been cut off from supplies, they lack food. (Cf. par. 80)
   2. When the ships arrive, we shall have enough men.
   3. When Cassius was preparing to leave camp, a sudden storm arose.
   4. Although all these things have happened, we shall not surrender.
   5. Finally, when Caesar had collected as many ships as possible, he attacked the smallest islands. (Cf. par. 80)
   6. Although we fear treachery, we shall not arrest him.
   7. When the general gives the signal, the soldiers advance.
   8. While the two armies were fighting it out, the inhabitants suffered from hunger.
   9. After having fled to the hills, the horsemen hid in the woods.
   10. When the war is finished, we shall go home.
   11. At the time when he found the money, he was a boy.
   12. Since he does not have suitable clothing, he says he will not go with us.
   13. When he returns, I shall depart for the country myself.
   14. Although those Germans had surrendered their arms, they hoped to defeat us.
   15. While searching for the king's beautiful daughter, we met the king himself.
   16. Since the river was not very deep, they were able to cross easily.
   17. When father comes home, he will give us something new.
   18. Caesar was our general when the Gauls were defeated.
   19. Since he has defeated many tribes, he will be called Imperator.
   20. When we were leaving the big city, we caught sight of that famous ship, the Queen Mary, approaching shore.
   21. But when I ask you to bring back the money, what will you do?
   22. When he goes to town, he buys many things for himself.
   23. After the enemy had been defeated, we freed the sea of the enemy's ships.
   24. Since they suspect nothing, we are safe.

25. Although he had always been a brave man, the silence of the place terrified him.
26. Brutus ought to be our leader, since he is so skilled in journeys of this kind.
27. When the king had collected a large army and was preparing to attack us, he suddenly formed a new plan.
28. Although he had arrived before daybreak, many men were waiting near the gates.
29. When we are in Rome, we ought to do the same things which the Romans do.
30. When their largest cities have been destroyed with this new kind of weapons, not even one inhabitant will survive.

LESSON XVII

The Gerund and Gerundive

82. *The Gerund* is a verbal noun, active, used in the *singular* only, in the Genitive, Dative, Accusative, and Ablative. The Infinitive takes the place of the missing Nominative.

> Nom. — (Laudāre, to praise, praising)
> Gen. — Laudandī, of praising
> Dat.— Laudandō, for praising
> Acc. — Laudandum, praising
> Abl. — Laudandō, by praising

83. *The Gerundive* is a verbal adjective, used in the *singular and plural* in all genders and cases (30 forms). Laudandus-a-um (For meanings and uses, see par. 85).

84.

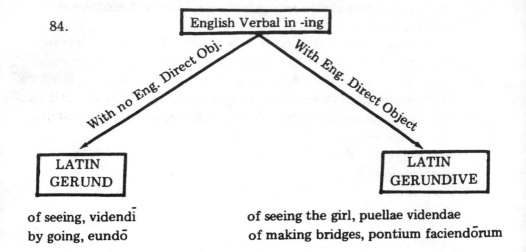

LATIN GERUND

of seeing, videndī
by going, eundō

LATIN GERUNDIVE

of seeing the girl, puellae videndae
of making bridges, pontium faciendōrum

But Latin Intransitives used with the Dative (Cf. par. 22) have the *Gerund* and keep the Dative.

of persuading them, eīs persuādendī

85. *Case Uses of the Gerund and Gerundive*:

(NOMINATIVE of Gerund is missing. Use Subjective Infinitive (Cf. par. 60))

Praising (To praise) is easy.
Laudāre est facile.

(NOMINATIVE of Gerundive. (Cf. Lesson XVIII))

GENITIVE of Gerund and Gerundive

(a) With Nouns and Adjectives
He was desirous of fighting.
Cupidus erat pugnandī.
A plan of making money, Consīlium pecūniae faciendae

(b) Followed by *Causā*, For the sake of, to express *Purpose*
For the sake of going, In order to go, Eundī causā

NOTE: With the following Pronouns in the Genitive: *Meī, Tuī, Suī, Nostrī,* and *Vestrī*, the Gerundive ends in *-ī* regardless of the gender and number of the Pronoun.

The girls did this for the sake of freeing themselves.
Puellae hoc fēcērunt suī līberandī causā.

4*TIVE* of Gerund and Gerundive, used with Adjectives meaning *Fit*, *Suitable*, and *Useful*.

Books suitable for reading, Librī idōneī legendō

ACCUSATIVE of Gerund and Gerundive, used with *Ad*, *for*, to express *Purpose*.

For making money (In order to make money), Ad pecūniam faciendam

ABLATIVE of Gerund and Gerundive, used in various Ablative constructions (with and without Prepositions)

By working, Labōrandō

About capturing the city, Dē expugnandā urbe

86. 1. For the sake of fleeing.
  2. By crossing the river.
  3. Weapons useful for fighting.
  4. In order to collect the baggage.
  5. By trusting him.
  6. The art of self defense
  7. He wished to learn about repairing ships.
  8. They had not yet made an end of talking.
  9. Large horses are suitable for carrying heavy burdens.
  10. You will accomplish nothing by resisting them.
  11. A few days were enough for building towers.
  12. They were not given the opportunity of recovering (their) weapons.
  13. Withstanding their attacks was most difficult.
  14. By killing all the enemy we shall destroy the fear of a new war.
  15. He had come for the purpose of harming the king.
  16. Girls, have you a plan of training yourselves?
  17. We put aside the hope of staying in the country that summer.
  18. By advancing quickly to the river our legion alarmed the enemy.
  19. He wrote a book about sailing.
  20. This place is not suitable for finding animals.
  21. Mother was desirous of saving herself.
  22. She adopted the plan of returning home.
  23. They had no reason for delaying longer.
  24. Talking is easy, but we cannot lessen the danger by talking.
  25. We prepared everything which had to do with attacking a town.
  26. He had no hope of defeating that nation.
  27. His men are very skilled in building towers.

28. The ships are ready for sailing.

29. He has the chance to spend the winter in Athens.

30. Collecting swords pleased him greatly.

31. He carried a large supply of money with him for the purpose of buying wine.

32. We can help others by obeying the laws.

33. Everything was done to please the soldiers.

34. Friends, I am saying this for the sake of encouraging you.

35. Have you seen the book which he wrote about the art of loving?

36. Time was not given for throwing javelins.

LESSON XVIII

The Passive Periphrastic

87. *The Passive Periphrastic*, a combination of the *Gerundive* and forms of *Sum*, expresses necessity or obligation. *Personal Agent* is expressed by the *Dative*.

> The money $\left. \begin{array}{l} \text{must} \\ \text{ought to} \\ \text{is to} \end{array} \right\}$ be found by you.

Pecūnia tibi reperienda est.

> The citizens $\left. \begin{array}{l} \text{had to} \\ \text{were to} \end{array} \right\}$ be warned by us.

Cīves nōbīs monendī erant (fuērunt).

Our ships will have to be repaired.

Nostrae nāvēs reficiendae erunt.

88. When the Passive Periphrastic is used, all *active* verbs in English must be turned into the *passive*:

   (a) *Transitive verbs* are used *Personally* in the passive.

   We must capture the city. The city must be captured by us.

   Urbs nōbīs expugnanda est.

   (b) *Intransitive verbs* are used *Impersonally* in the passive (Cf. par. 23).

   We must set out. (It) must be set out by us.

   Nōbīs proficiscendum est.

42

We ought to obey the laws. (It) ought to be obeyed to the laws by us.
Nōbis parendum est lēgibus.

(1) When two Datives (a Dative of the Agent and a Dative with a Special Verb, Cf. par. 22) would cause ambiguity, *Personal Agent* is expressed by *Ab* (*ā*) + *Ablative.*

We must persuade them. (It) must be persuaded to them by us.
Eīs ā nōbīs persuādendum est.

(2) Notice that impersonal *It* is not expressed in Latin.

(3) Notice that in the *impersonal* use of the Passive Periphrastic, the Gerundive always ends in *-dum.*

89. The Passive Periphrastic is frequently used in *Indirect Statements* and *Indirect Questions.*

> I know that the city must be captured.
> Sciō urbem expugnandam esse.
> He asked what must be done.
> Rogāvit quid faciendum esset.

90. 1. Two cohorts must be sent.
  2. Our army must defend the city.
  3. We must flee.
  4. You ought to trust me, my friend.
  5. He thinks that the women should be left at home.
  6. The soldiers must not go far from camp.
  7. A larger supply of food should be sent.
  8. I know what river we must cross.
  9. Those trees will have to be moved.
  10. We ought to resist the Germans.
  11. You must not come nearer, Anna.
  12. Those boys had to run home.
  13. We must approach the enemy's camp carefully.
  14. Caesar had to choose a new route.
  15. Our allies must be trusted.
  16. These girls have to read many books.
  17. We must not delay longer.
  18. Men who lack money should not be despised.
  19. We must not complain.
  20. The tenth legion must be praised.
  21. They will have to cross without boats.

22. Ambassadors ought not to be harmed.

23. Then she said that she must depart.

24. The enemy must be given no time to move camp.

25. We must take away all hope of returning home.

26. American soldiers have often had to fight with Germans.

27. Because of this he had to leave town.

28. The wretched captives must be spared.

29. Many men will have to die in this battle.

30. Don't you understand why the booty must be returned?

31. We must trust our friends.

32. Caesar had to put Brutus in command of the cavalry.

33. You must urge him not to lose the hope of finding his daughter.

34. Water must be carried to the wounded men.

protasis — if

apodosis — main

LESSON XIX

Conditional Sentences, Simple and Future

91. Conditional Sentences are composed of two parts:
   (a) *The Condition*, a subordinate clause introduced by one of the
       following:
       If, *Sī*
       Unless, *Nisi*
       But if, *Quod sī* or *Sīn*
   NOTE: After *Sī, Nisi, Num* or *Nē*, every *ali-* drops away from *aliquis,*
   aliquid, someone, anyone, something, anything, and from *aliquī, aliqua,*
   aliquod, some, any.
       If he sees anything, he will return.
       Sī quid vīderit, redibit.
   (b) *The Conclusion*, the main clause of the sentence.

44

92.

		CONDITION	CONCLUSION
		Indicative, Present or Past	Indicative, Present or Past
Simple		If he is running Sī currit If he ran Sī cucurrit	he is winning. superat. he won. superāvit.
Future	More definite	Indicative, Future or Future Perf. (Completed)	Indicative, Future
		If he runs Sī curret If he wins (shall have won) Sī superāverit	he will win. superābit. he will receive the prize. praemium accipiet.
	Less definite	Subjunctive, Present or Perfect (Completed)	Subjunctive, Present
		If he should run Sī currat If he should win (should have won) Sī superāverit	he would win. superet. he would receive the prize. praemium accipiat.

[handwritten annotations: "vivid" (More definite), "vivid" (Less definite), "should-would"]

93. 1. If I survive, I shall return home.

2. If you were in Rome at that time, you were safe.

3. But if we should return, he would harm us.

4. If our legions are routed, they will flee to the river. (Cf. par. 80)

5. If anyone is tired, he hinders the others.

6. I will kill you if you move your hands.

7. Unless you give him something, he will not bring the food.

8. If Anna should deceive me, I would immediately look for another girl.

9. But if you are afraid to fight, this is not a suitable place for you.

10. If any ships are destroyed, we shall be in danger.

11. I will help you if you are unable to finish the work.

12. Unless something is done, we shall soon have no food.

13. If you were to (should) go to the same place, you would find many stones of this kind.

14. If Brutus lived in that valley, he saw the mountains daily.

15. But if any chance is given him, he will deceive us.

16. If Marcus should win, he would be worthy of praise.
17. I will not allow you to go, my son, unless you return these books.
18. Unless something new (Cf. par. 9) is said, most men will depart.
19. What would you say if he should try to find you, lieutenant?
20. If anyone touches me, I shall shout.
21. If you look at the sun with (your) eyes open, you will be able to see nothing afterward.
22. If you think that your javelins are heavy, Marcus, you ought to lift mine.
23. If they do not reach camp at sunset, we shall send men to search for them.
24. But if the general were to divide the booty, all of us would have a small part.
25. Unless the hostages go with us, they will all perish within a short time.

LESSON XX

Conditional Sentences, Contrary to Fact

94.

		CONDITION	CONCLUSION
Contrary to Fact	Present Time	*Imperfect Subjunctive* If he were running Sī curreret	*Imperfect Subjunctive* he would be winning. superāret.
	Past Time	*Pluperfect Subjunctive* If he had run Sī cucurrisset	*Pluperfect Subjunctive* he would have won. superāvisset.

95. *Contrary to Fact* conditional sentences have the following irregularities:
   (a) A *Past* Contrary to Fact condition (Plup. Subjv.) may have a present conclusion (Imperfect Subjv.).
   If we had left earlier, we would be at home now.
   Sī mātūrius discessissēmus, nunc domī essēmus.
   (b) When the verb of the *conclusion* of a Contrary to Fact conditional sentence is *Possum*, or expresses any idea of *necessity* (*Dēbeō* or the Passive Periphrastic), that verb is often *Indicative*. In this use, the *Im-*

46

perfect Indicative replaces the *Imperfect Subjunctive*, the *Perfect Indicative* replaces the *Pluperfect Subjunctive*.

If he were present, he ought to be praised.

Sī adesset, laudandus erat.

If he had run, he could have won.

Sī cucurrisset, superāre potuit.

96. 1. If this road were wider, we would be proceeding faster.
2. Had they set fire to one of the buildings, the whole village would have been destroyed.
3. If scouts are sent ahead, they will learn the enemy's plans.
4. If he is working, he is making money.
5. If you had enough money, you could buy the mountain.
6. Unless someone sends help, we shall all die.
7. Marcus would be a free man today if he had not stolen the general's money.
8. What would you have done if he had tried to drag you to the swamp?
9. But if he does not wish to stay, why does he hesitate to depart?
10. If he had said anything, he would have been deprived of liberty.
11. If we knew his plans, we could resist him.
12. Unless someone complains, the pay will not be increased.
13. Had he been wounded, we would have had to depart.
14. If you should summon him, he would not be able to come.
15. But if we had arrested him at that time, he would not be so powerful now.
16. If that stone were heavier, I could not lift it.
17. If Anna had been able to go, she would have been very happy.
18. If the girls wander along the shore, they will find the wrecked ship.
19. Were Caesar alive today, he would be surprised at many things.
20. But if a storm should arise, our ships would be driven back to the harbor.
21. They would not have found the places if they had not descended from the hills.
22. If we seize the harbor, the enemy's fleet will be unable to attack our island.
23. Had I dared to open the gates, I could have deceived the guards.
24. If any chance is given, you ought to carry the wounded men out of danger.

25. If this lady were lighter, I would be able to carry her to the top of the hill.
26. Unless we put another leader in charge of our army, we shall be crushed in a short time.
27. If you had intrusted your safety to me, Cassius, you would now be at home with your friends.
28. If anyone were to praise him, he would reply that he is unworthy of praise.
29. You would have seen the whole army, my friends, if you had remained on that hill.
30. I shall be happy if he returns before midnight.

CONNECTED PROSE

(For use after completion of all twenty lessons)

97. There was a certain town in Gaul which the Romans had never attacked. The inhabitants were so brave that they did not fear Caesar himself. They thought that he would not dare to approach the walls of their town. After learning this, Caesar sent one legion to capture the town. Within a few hours, the inhabitants of the town were defeated and asked the Roman soldiers not to kill them.
98. Then the general asked certain of the guards to depart from the council so that all could see the captured king more easily. Since this king was a man of great courage, many citizens had assembled. These men said that the king ought to be killed because he had made war on the Roman people. Suddenly however, the king, having snatched a weapon, wounded the general on the head and escaped. Although many men were sent to search for the king, they could not find him.
99. Our men did not want to advance at this time because they thought that the enemy would suddenly attack them. The lieutenant said that he would lead them to a river which they could cross. While the lieutenant was saying this, he was wounded by a heavy weapon. He was carried to the rear, but the men, fearing an ambush, set out as quickly as they could in order to reach home before night.
100. Caesar immediately ordered his men to burn the bridge. After doing this, he allowed the ambassadors of the Helvetians to come to him. He told them that he wished to wait a few days in order to decide what

must be done about this matter. But when the ambassadors had departed, Caesar ordered his men to fortify the place. This was done so speedily that the Helvetians were prevented from marching through our province.

101. While Caesar was preparing to return to Rome, he put a certain lieutenant in command of the camp. He warned this man not to attack the enemy, for he feared that the Roman legions would be defeated. After Caesar had departed, this lieutenant saw that a few of the enemy were advancing to the Roman camp. Since he wished to learn what they were doing, he ordered his cavalry to follow them. The enemy however, quickly collected reinforcements, defeated the horsemen, and killed them.

102. "Do not urge us to stay here with you, good Cassius," replied the lieutenant. "This place is a little higher than the river, but I fear that we shall not be able to resist the enemy. Believe me, my friend, I am skilled in matters of this kind. I tell you that we shall be driven out easily within a few days. Let us not pitch camp here, but let us depart quickly in order that no one may see us." Alarmed by this speech, Cassius sent ahead certain of his scouts to choose a better place.

103. Having proceeded three miles into the territory of the Germans, our general ordered his men to pitch camp in this place. Since he knew that the enemy were approaching with great speed, he thought that they would make an attack before sunset. So quickly was everything completed by our men that the enemy were unable to learn where we had halted. On the next day the enemy's troops were seen drawn up on the top of a hill. Our general, having encouraged his men by a short speech, gave the signal for battle. The enemy were routed by the first attack of our brave footsoldiers and fled home.

104. After getting possession of the town, our general warned the inhabitants to surrender all their arms immediately. Certain of the inhabitants, terrified by the speech of the general, thought that they ought to do what he asked. Others however were afraid that if they surrendered their arms, they would become slaves of the Romans. Since they did not know what they should do about this, they finally decided to hide part of their arms. When our general learned this, he drove out the inhabitants and burned the town.

105. In order that no one might say that our men lacked courage, the lieutenant led three cohorts out of the city and attacked the enemy at day-

break. Although he was surpassed in number of men, he easily routed the enemy. Having gained possession of much booty, he returned to Rome. After the citizens learned these things, they said that the lieutenant was worthy of the greatest praise. If the lieutenant had not been skilled in war, he could not have defeated so large a multitude of the enemy.

106. Two of the ships had been driven back to the island by a storm. The Roman soldiers had to remain on the island all night. They had to do many things: the ships had to be repaired, food had to be found, new plans had to be formed. They were not given the opportunity of completing this work however, for in the middle of the night the Britons made a fierce attack. "We must resist the enemy bravely," shouted the lieutenant. The enemy were finally defeated, and at daybreak the Romans lifted anchor and left the island.

107. A certain general who was besieging a town warned the inhabitants not to go out from the walls. After the town was captured, he sent a lieutenant to find whether the inhabitants had obeyed him. The lieutenant reported that two of the enemy's chiefs had escaped so quickly during the night that they could not be caught. Upon learning this, the general sent his cavalry to overtake them. The chiefs were caught and brought back to the town. They have lost all hope of escaping again.

108. Although the Germans had seized the most beautiful city of Italy, they were finally driven out however by the bravery of our allies. American soldiers who were sent to that famous city found that many buildings had been destroyed by the Germans. The inhabitants, terrified by the war, remained at home and did not dare to go out into the streets because they feared that they would be harmed. But when these citizens learned that American soldiers had arrived for the purpose of freeing the city, they were greatly delighted. They said that a large part of the city which had been devastated must be repaired. They knew that our men would be a great help to them. If you should go to this city, you would see that many buildings have been repaired.

VOCABULARY

A

able (be), possum, posse, potuī,
—————

about, dē (prep. with abl.)

accomplish, cōnficiō-ere, cōnfēci,
cōnfectus

across, built a bridge across, pon-
tem facere in (w. abl.)

added to this is the fact, additur
(cf. par. 73)

advance, prōcēdō-ere, prōcessī,
prōcessum; prōgredior-i, prō-
gressus

advantage, auxilium-ī, n. (cf. par.
18); ūsus-ūs, m. (cf. par. 18)

advantageous, auxiliō; ūsuī
(cf. par. 18)

advise, moneō-ēre, monuī, monitus

afraid (be), timeō-ēre, timuī,
— —; vereor-ēri, veritus

after, cum

afterward, posteā (adv.)

again, iterum (adv.)

against my will, mē invitō

alarm, permoveō-ēre, permōvī,
permōtus

alive, vīvus-a-um; be alive, vīvō-
ere, vīxī, —————

all, omnis-e

allow, patior-i, passus; permittō-
ere, permīsi, permissus

ally, socius-ī, m.

alone, sōlus-a-um

along, per (prep. w. acc.)

already, iam

although, cum

always, semper

ambassador, lēgātus-ī, m.

ambush, insidiae-ārum, f.

American, Americānus-a-um; an
American, Americānus-ī, m.

anchor, ancora-ae, f.

animal, animal-ālis, n.

Anna, Anna-ae, f.

announce, nūntiō, 1

Antonius, Antōnius-ī, m.

any, aliquī, aliqua, aliquod

anyone, aliquis

approach, appropinquō, 1

arise, orior, orīri, ortus

arms, arma-ōrum, n.

army, exercitus-ūs, m.

arrest, comprehendō-ere, com-
prehendī, comprehēnsus

arrival, adventus-ūs, m.

arrive at, perveniō-ire, pervēnī,
perventum ad (w. acc)

arrow, sagitta-ae, f.

art, ars, artis, f.

as many as possible, quam
plūrimī-ae-a

as soon as possible, quam prī-
mum (adv.)

ask, rogo, 1; quaerō-ere, quaesīvī,
quaesitus

assemble, conveniō-ire, convēni,
conventum

Athens, Athēnae-ārum, f.

attack, impetus-ūs, m.

attack, oppugnō, 1 (of towns,
etc.); petō-ere, petīvī, petitus
(of persons)

await, exspectō, 1

B

bad, malus-a-um

baggage, impedīmenta-ōrum, n.

bank, rīpa-ae, f.

battle, proelium-ī, n.

be, sum, esse, fuī, futūrus

beach, subdūcō-ere, subdūxī, subductus

beautiful, pulcher-chra-chrum

because, quod

because of, ob; propter (preps. w. acc.)

become, fīō, fierī, factus

before, ante (prep. w. acc.)

began, coepī, coeptus (in perf. system only)

behind, post (prep. w. acc.)

believe, crēdō-ere, crēdidī, crēditum

besiege, obsideō-ēre, obsēdī, obsessus

betake one's self, sē cōnferō, cōnferre, contulī, collātus

Bibulus, Bibulus-ī, m.

boat, nāvigium-ī, n.

body, corpus-oris, n.

boldly, audācter

book, liber, librī, m.

booty, praeda-ae, f.

boy, puer, puerī, m.

brave, fortis-e

bravery, virtūs-ūtis, f.

break, frangō-ere, frēgī, frāctus

bridge, pōns, pontis, m.

bring, ferō, ferre, tulī, lātus

bring back, reducō-ere, redūxī, reductus; referō, referre, rettulī, relātus

bring in, importō, 1

bring it about, efficiō-ere, effēcī, effectus; faciō-ere, fēcī, factus; perficiō-ere, perfēcī, perfectus (cf. par. 73)

bring together, cōnferō, cōnferre, contulī, collātus

British (the), Britannī-ōrum, m.

Briton (a), Britannus-ī, m.

broad, lātus-a-um

brother, frāter, frātris, m.

Brutus, Brūtus-ī, m.

build, faciō-ere, fēcī, factus

building, aedificium-ī, n.

burden, onus-eris, n.

burn, incendō-ere, incendī, incēnsus

but, sed

but if, quod sī; sīn

buy, emō-ere, ēmī, ēmptus

by, ā, ab

C

Caesar, Caesar-aris, m.

call, vocō, 1

camp, castra-ōrum, n.

can, possum, posse, potuī, ————

captive, captīvus-ī, m.

capture, capiō-ere, cēpī, captus

care, cūra-ae, f. (cf. par. 18)

carry, portō, 1

Cassius, Cassius-ī, m.

catch, excipiō-ere, excēpī, exceptus

catch sight of, cōnspiciō-ere, cōnspēxī, cōnspectus

cause, causa-ae, f.

cause (something to be done),
efficiō-ere, effēcī, effectus;
faciō-ere, fēcī, factus; perficiō-
ere, perfēcī, perfectus (cf. par.
73)

cavalry, equitēs-um, m.

cavalryman, eques, equitis, m.

certain, quīdam, quaedam, quod-
dam or quiddam

chance, facultās-ātis, f.

chief, prīnceps-cipis, m.

children, līberī-ōrum, m.

choose, dēligō-ere, dēlēgi, dēlec-
tus

citizen, cīvis, cīvis, m.

city, urbs, urbis, f.

close, claudō-ere, clausī, clausus

clothing, vestis, vestis, f.

cohort, cohors, cohortis, f.

collect, colligō-ere, collēgī, col-
lectus

come, veniō-īre, vēnī, ventum

command (be in command of),
praesum, praeesse, praefuī,
praefutūrus (cf. par. 21b)

complain, queror-ī, questus

complete, cōnficiō-ere, cōnfēcī,
cōnfectus

conspiracy, coniūratiō-ōnis, f.

consul, cōnsul, cōnsulis, m.

consulship (cf. par. 56)

council, concilium-ī, n.

country, rūs, rūris, n. (opposite
of city); patria-ae, f. (native
land)

courage, virtūs, virtūtis, f.

cross, trānseō, trānsīre, trānsiī,
trānsitūrus

crush, opprimō-ere, oppressī,
oppressus

custom, mōs, mōris, m.

cut off, interclūdō-ere, interclūsī,
interclūsus

D

daily, cōttidiē

danger, perīculum-ī, n.

dare, audeō-ēre, ausus

daughter, fīlia-ae, f.

day, dies, diēī, m. (f.)

daybreak, prīma lūx, prīmae
lūcis, f.

deceive, fallō-ere, fefellī, falsus

decide, cōnstituō-ere, cōnstituī,
cōnstitūtus

deep, altus-a-um

defeat, vincō-ere, vīcī, victus

defend, dēfendō-ere, dēfendī,
dēfēnsus

delay, mora-ae, f.

delay, moror, 1

delight, dēlectō, 1

demand, poscō-ere, poposcī,
———

depart, discēdō-ere, discessī, discessūrus

departure, discessus-ūs, m.

deprive of, prīvō, 1 (cf. par. 32b,
Note)

depth, altitūdō-inis, f.

descend, dēscendō-ere, dēscendi, dēscēnsus

desire, cupiō-ere, cupivi, cupitus

desirous, cupidus-a-um

despise, dēspiciō-ere, dēspexi, dēspectus

destroy, dēleō-ēre, dēlēvi, dēlētus

devastate, populor, 1; vāstō, 1

die, morior, mori, mortuus (moritūrus)

difficult, difficilis-e

diligently, dīligenter

disaster, calamitās-ātis, f.

disgraceful, turpis-e

dismiss, dīmittō-ere, dīmisi, dīmissus

ditch, fossa-ae, f.

divide, dīvidō-ere, dīvisi, dīvisus

do, faciō-ere, fēci, factus

drag, trahō-ere, trāxi, trāctus

draw up, īnstruō-ere, īnstrūxi, instrūctus

drive back, repellō-ere, reppuli, repulsus

drive out, expellō-ere, expuli, expulsus

E

eager, avidus-a-um; cupidus-a-um

eagle, aquila-ae, f.

easily, facile (adv.)

easy, facilis-e

eight, octō

encourage, cohortor, 1; cōnfirmō, 1

end, fīnis, fīnis, m.

end of, extrēmus-a-um

enemy, hostis, hostis, m.

enjoy, fruor-i, frūctus (cf. par. 35a)

enough, satis (cf. par. 9)

escape, effugiō-ere, effūgi, ——

ever, umquam

everything, omnia-ium, n.

expect, exspectō, 1

expel, expellō-ere, expuli, expulsus

eye, oculus-i, m.

F

fail, dēsum, dēesse, dēfui, dēfutūrus (w. dat.); dēficiō-ere, dēfēci, dēfectus (w. acc.)

fall, cadō-ere, cecidi, cāsūrus

famous (that), ille, illa, illud (after its noun)

far, longē

farmer, agricola-ae, m.

fast, celer, celeris, celere (adj.); celeriter (adv.)

father, pater, patris, m.

fear, timor-ōris, m.

fear, timeō-ēre, timui, ——; vereor-ēri, veritus

few, pauci-ae-a

field, ager, agri, m.

fierce, ācer, ācris, ācre
fight, pugnō, 1
fight it out, dēcertō, 1
fill, compleō-ere, complēvī, com-
plētus
finally, tandem
find, reperiō-īre, repperī, repertus
finish, cōnficiō-ere, cōnfēcī, cōnfectus
first, prīmus-a-um
five, quīnque
flee, fugiō-ere, fūgī, ———
fleet, classis-is, f.
flight, fuga-ae, f.
Florence, Flōrentia-ae, f.
Florida, Flōrida-ae, f.
follow, sequor-ī, secūtus
food, cibus-ī, m.
foot, pēs, pedis, m.
foot of (at the), sub (prep. w.
abl.)

footsoldier, pedes, peditis, m.
for, in behalf of, prō (prep. w.
abl.)
for a long time, diū
force, vīs, vīs, f.
forest, silva-ae, f.
form a plan, cōnsilium capiō-ere,
cēpī, captus
fort, castellum-ī, n.
fortifications, moenia-ium, n.
fortify, mūniō-īre, mūnīvī, mūnī-
tus
four, quattuor
France, Gallia-ae, f.
free, līber-era-erum
free, līberō, 1
freedom, lībertās-ātis, f.
friend, amīcus-ī, m.
friendly, amīcus-a-um
frighten, terreō-ēre, terruī, territus
from, ā, ab; ē, ex; dē

G

gain possession of, potior-īrī,
potītus (cf. par. 35a)
gate, porta-ae, f.
Gaul, Gallia-ae, f. (the country);
Gallus-ī, m. (a Gaul)
general, dux, ducis, m.; imperā-
tor-ōris, m.
German (a), Germānus-ī, m.
get possession of, potior-īrī,
potītus (cf. par. 35a)
gift, dōnum-ī, n.

girl, puella-ae, f.
give, dō, dare, dedī, datus
go, eo, īre, iī, itūrus
go away, discēdō-ere, discessī,
discessūrus
go out, exeō, exīre, exiī, exitūrus
good, bonus-a-um
gratitude, grātia-ae, f.
greatly, magnopere
guard, praesidium-ī, n.; custōs,
custōdis, m. (a sentinel)

H

halt, cōnsistō-ere, cōnstitī, ———
hand, manus-ūs, f.
hand over, trādō-ere, trādidī, trāditus
happen, fīō, fierī, factus
happens (it), accidit; fit (cf. par. 73)
happy, laetus-a-um
harass, lacessō-ere, lacessīvī, lacessītus
harbor, portūs-us, m.
harm, noceō-ēre, nocuī, nocitūrus
hasten, mātūrō, 1 (w. inf.); contendō-ere, contendī, contentum (to a place)
have, habeō-ēre, habuī, habitus
have to do with, pertineō-ēre, pertinuī, ———, ad (w. acc.)
head, caput, capitis, n.
hear, audiō-īre, audīvī, audītus
heavy, gravis-e
help, auxilium-ī, n. (cf. par. 18)
help, iuvō-āre, iūvī, iūtus
Helvetians, Helvētiī-ōrum, m.
her, suus-a-um (reflex. adj.); eius (non-reflex. pronoun) (cf. par. 25, 26)

here, hīc (in this place); hūc (to this place)
hesitate, dubitō, 1
hide, abdō-ere, abdidī, abditus
high, altus-a-um
hill, collis-is, m.
himself, suī (reflex.); ipse (non-reflex.) (cf. par. 25, 26, Note)
hinder, impediō-īre, impedīvī, impedītus
hindrance, impedimentum-ī, n. (cf. par. 18)
his, suus-a-um (reflex. adj.); eius (non-reflex. pronoun) (cf. par. 25, 26)
hold, teneō-ēre, tenuī, ———
home, domus-ūs, f. (cf. par. 33)
hope, spēs, speī, f.
hope, spērō, 1
horse, equus-ī, m.
horseman, eques, equitis, m.
hostage, obses, obsidis, m.
hour, hōra-ae, f.
house, domus-ūs, f.
however, tamen
hunger, famēs-is, f.

I

I, ego
if, sī
immediately, statim
in, in (prep. w. abl.)
in order not to, nē
in order to, ut
increase, augeō-ēre, auxī, auctus
infantry, peditēs-um, m.
influence, auctōritās-ātis, f.

inform, certiōrem faciō-ere, fecī, factus (certior agrees w. obj.)
informed (be), certior fīō, fierī, factus (certior agrees w. subj.)
inhabitant, incola-ae, m.
intrust, mandō, 1
island, īnsula-ae, f.
Italy, Ītalia-ae, f.

J

javelin, pīlum-ī, n.
journey, iter, itineris, n.
just, iūstus-a-um

K

keep (from), prohibeō-ēre, prohibuī, prohibitus (cf. par. 32b)
keep still, taceō-ēre, tacuī, tacitum
kill, interficiō-ere, interfēci, interfectus; necō, 1
kind, genus-eris, n. modus-ī, m.

king, rēx, rēgis, m.
know, sciō-īre, scīvī, scītus; cog-
   nōvi (in perfect system means
   know, have learned); not
know, nesciō-īre, nescīvī, ――――

L

Labienus, Labiēnus-ī, m.
lack, inopia-ae, f.
lack, careō-ēre, caruī, caritūrus
   (cf. par. 32b, Note)
lady, fēmina-ae, f.
land, terra-ae, f.
large, magnus-a-um
law, lex, lēgis, f.
lead, dūcō-ere, dūxī, ductus
lead back, redūcō-ere, redūxī,
   reductus
lead out, edūcō-ere, ēdūxī, ēduc-
   tus
leader, dux, ducis, m.
leadership (cf. par. 56)
learn, cognōscō-ere, cognōvī,
   cognitus
leave, relinquō-ere, relīquī, relic-
   tus (w. acc.)
legion, legiō-ōnis, f.
less, minus

lessen, minuō-ere, minuī, minūtus
letter, litterae-ārum, f.
liberty, libertās-ātis, f.
lieutenant, lēgātus-ī, m.
life, vīta-ae, f.
lift, tollō-ere, sustulī, sublātus
light, levis-e
like, similis-e
listen, audiō-īre, audīvī, audītus
little, parvus-a-um
little, by a little, paulō (adv.)
long, longus-a-um
longer, diūtius (adv.)
look at, aspiciō-ere, aspexī,
   aspectus
look for, quaerō-ere, quaesīvī,
   quaesītus
lose, amittō-ere, amīsī, amissus
love, amor, amōris, m.
love, amō, 1

M

made (be), fīō, fierī, factus
make, faciō-ere, fēcī, factus
make an attack on, impetum
   facere in (w. acc.)
make war on, bellum īnferō,
   īnferre, intulī, illātus (cf. par.
   21b)
man, vir, virī, m.
many, multī-ae-a
march, contendō-ere, contendī,
   contentum
Marcus, Mārcus-ī, m.
Mary, Marīa-ae, f.
master, dominus-ī, m.
matter, rēs, reī, f.
meet, occurrō-ere, occurrī,
   occursūrus (cf. par. 21b)
merchant, mercātor-ōris, m.
middle of, medius-a-um

midnight, media nox, mediae
   noctis, f.
mile, mīlle passūs; miles, mīlia
   passuum
mine, meus-a-um
money, pecūnia-ae, f.
month, mēnsis-is, m.
moon, lūna-ae, f.
more, plūs (adv. of amount);
   magis (adv. of degree); amplius
   (longer, further)
most, plērīque, plēraeque, plēra-
   que
mother, māter, mātris, f.
mountain, mōns, montis, m.
move, moveō-ēre, mōvī, mōtus
multitude, multitūdō-inis, f.
my, meus-a-um

N

name, nōmen-inis, n.
nation, nātiō-ōnis, f.
nature, nātūra-ae, f.
near, propinquus-a-um (cf. par.
   19); ad (prep. w. acc.)
nearer, propius (adv.)
neighboring, fīnitimus-a-um
never, numquam
new, novus-a-um
next, proximus-a-um
night, nox, noctis, f.

no, nūllus-a-um; nihil (cf. par. 9)
nobody, nēmō (acc. nēminem)
not, nōn; nē; ut (after verbs of
   fearing)
not even, nē . . . quidem
not yet, nōndum
nothing, nihil
now, nunc
number, numerus-ī, m.; (a great)
   number, multitūdō-inis, f.

O

obey, pareō-ēre, paruī, ———
  (cf. par. 22)
obtain, obtineō-ēre, obtinuī,
  obtentus
often, saepe
older, maior natū, maiōris nātū
on, in (prep. w. abl.)
one, ūnus-a-um
open, aperiō-īre, aperuī, apertus
opportunity, occasiō-ōnis, f.

order, iubeō-ēre, iussī, iussus (Cf.
  par. 72 Note); imperō, 1 (Cf.
  par. 22, 72)
other, alter-era-erum (the other
  of two); alius-a-ud (other,
  another)
ought, dēbeō-ēre, dēbuī, dēbitus
our, noster-tra-trum
out of, dē (prep. w. abl.)
overtake, cōnsequor-ī, cōnsecūtus

P

pardon, ignōscō-ere, ignōvī, ignō-
  tum (cf. par. 22)
part, pars, partis, f.
pay, stīpendium-ī, n.
peace, pāx, pācis, f.
perish, pereō-īre, periī, peritūrus
persuade, persuādeō-ēre, persuāsī,
  persuāsum (cf. par. 22, 72)
pitch camp, castra pōnere
place, locus-ī, m. (pl. loca-ōrum,
  n.)
plan, cōnsilium-i, n.; adopt a
  plan, cōnsilium capere
please, placeō-ēre, placuī, placi-
  tum (cf. par. 22)
pleasing, grātus-a-um
possessions, rēs, rērum, f. Neuter
  pl. of possessive adj. (mea, tua,
  sua, etc.)
powerful, potēns, potentis
praise, laus, laudis, f.

praise, laudō, 1
pray, ōrō, 1
prefer, mālō, mālle, māluī, ———
prepare, parō, 1
pretty, pulcher-chra-chrum
prevent, prohibeō-ēre, prohibuī,
  prohibitus (cf. par. 59e)
proceed, prōcēdō-ēre, prōcessī,
  prōcessūrus; prōgredior-ī, prō-
  gressus
promise, polliceor-ērī, pollicitus
province, prōvincia-ae, f.
purpose of (for the), causā (preceded by gen.)
put, pōnō-ere, posuī, positus
put aside, dēpōnō-ere, dēposuī,
  dēpositus
put in command of, praeficiō-ere,
  praefēci, praefectus (cf. par.
  21b)

Q

queen, rēgina-ae, f.
quickly, celeriter

R

rampart, vallum-ī, n.

reach, perveniō-īre, pervēnī, perventum ad (w. acc.)

read, legō-ere, lēgī, lēctus

ready, parātus-a-um

rear, novissimum agmen, novissimī agminis, n.

reason, causa-ae, f.

receive, recipiō-ere, recēpī, receptus

recover, recuperō, 1

region, regiō-ōnis, f.

reinforcement, subsidium-ī, n.

remain, maneō-ēre, mānsī, mānsūrus

remember, meminī, meminisse (in perfect system only)

repair, reficiō-ere, refēcī, refectus

reply, respondeō-ēre, respondī, respōnsus

report, nūntiō, 1

repulse, repellō-ere, reppulī, repulsus

resist, resistō-ere, restitī, ———— (cf. par. 22)

rest of, reliquus-a-um

return, reddō-ere, reddidī, redditus (give back); redeō-īre, rediī, reditūrus (go back)

reward, praemium-ī, n.

Rhone, Rhodanus-i, m.

river, flūmen-inis, n.

road, iter, itineris, n.; via-ae, f.

Roman, Rōmānus-a-um; a Roman, Rōmānus-ī, m.

Rome, Rōma-ae, f.

rout, fugō, 1

route, iter, itineris, n.

run, currō-ere, cucurrī, cursūrus

S

safe, tūtus-a-um

safety, salūs-ūtis, f.

sail, nāvigō, 1

sailor, nauta-ae, m.

sake of (for the), causā (preceded by gen.)

same, īdem, eadem, idem

save, servō, 1

say, dīcō-ere, dīxī, dictus

say . . . not, negō, 1

scout, explōrātor-ōris, m.

sea, mare, maris, n.

search for, quaerō-ere, quaesivī, quaesītus

see, videō-ēre, vīdī, vīsus

seem, videor

seize, occupō, 1; capiō-ere, cēpī, captus (of persons)

-self, ipse, ipsa, ipsum (cf. par. 26, Note)

send, mittō-ere, mīsī, missus

send ahead, praemittō-ere, praemīsī, praemissus

serve, serviō-īre, servīvī, servitum (cf. par. 22)

set fire to, incendō-ere, incendī, incensus (w. acc.)

set out, proficiscor-ī, profectus

seven, septem

severely, graviter

shield, scūtum-ī, n.

ship, nāvis, nāvis, f.

60

shore, lītus, lītoris, n.
short, brevis-e
shout, clāmor, clāmōris, m.
shout, clāmō, 1
sick, aeger-gra-grum
signal, signum-ī, n.
silence, silentium-ī, n.
since, cum
skilled in, perītus-a-um (cf. par.
  19 Note)
slaughter, caedēs, caedis, f.
slave, servus-ī, m.
small, parvus-a-um
snatch, ēripiō-ere, ēripuī, ēreptus
so, ita; sīc; tam (cf. par. 69 Note)
so great, tantus-a-um
so many, tot
soldier, mīles, mīlitis, m.
something, aliquid (cf. par. 9)
son, fīlius-ī, m.
soon, mox
spare, parcō-ere, peperci, parsūrus
  (cf. par. 22)
spear, hasta-ae, f.
speech, ōrātiō-ōnis, f.
speed, celeritās-ātis, f.
spend the winter, hiemō, 1
start, proficīscor-ī, profectus
state, civitās-ātis, f.
stay, maneō-ēre, mānsī, mānsūrus
steal, auferō, auferre, abstulī,
  ablātus

stone, lapis, lapidis, m.
storm, tempestās-ātis, f.
story, fābula-ae, f.
street, via-ae, f.
struggle, contendō-ere, contendī,
  contentum
sudden, subitus-a-um
suddenly, subitō
suffer, labōrō, 1
suitable, idōneus-a-um
summer, aestās, aestātis, f.
summon, vocō, 1; convocō, 1
sun, sōl, sōlis, m.
sunset, sōlis occāsus, sōlis occāsus, m.
supplies, commeātus-ūs, m.
supply, cōpia-ae, f.
surpass, superō, 1
surprised at (be), mīror, 1
surrender, dēdō-ere, dēdidī,
  dēditus; trādō-ere, trādidī,
  trāditus
survive, supersum-esse-fuī-futūrus
suspect, suspicor, 1
swamp, palūs, palūdis, f.
swift, celer-eris-ere; vēlōx, vēlōcis
  (gen.)
sword, gladius-ī, m.
Syracuse, Syrācūsae-ārum, f.

T

take away, auferō, auferre, abstulī, ablātus
talk, loquor-ī, locūtus
tell, dīcō-ere, dīxī, dictus; nārrō, 1

ten, decem
tenth, decimus-a-um
terrify, terreō-ēre, terruī, territus
territory, fīnēs-ium, m.

than, quam (cf. par. 40)

that, ille, illa, illud

that famous, ille, illa, illud (after its noun)

their, suus-a-um (reflex. adj.); eōrum, eārum (non-reflex. pronoun) (cf. par. 25, 26)

then, tum

thing, rēs, reī, f.

think, existimō, 1; arbitror, 1; putō, 1

this, hīc, haec, hoc; is, ea, id

thousand, mīlle (pl. mīlia, mīlium)

threaten, minor, 1 (cf. par. 22)

three, trēs, tria

through, per (prep. w. acc.)

throw, iaciō-ere, iēcī, iactus

time, tempus, temporis, n.

tired, dēfessus-a-um

today, hodiē

top of, summus-a-um

touch, tangō-ere, tetigī, tāctus

tower, turris-is, f.

town, oppidum-ī, n.

train, exercitō, 1

treachery, perfidia-ae, f.

tree, arbor, arboris, f.

tribe, gēns, gentis, f.

troops, cōpiae-ārum, f.

trust, cōnfidō-ere, cōnfisus; crēdō-ere, crēdidī, crēditum (cf. par. 22)

try, cōnor, 1; temptō, 1

Tullius, Tullius-ī, m.

twelve, duodecim

twenty, vīgintī

two, duo, duae, duo

U

under, sub (prep. w. abl.)

understand, intellegō-ere, intellēxī, intellēctus

undertake, suscipiō-ere, suscēpi, susceptus

unfriendly, inimīcus-a-um (cf. par. 19)

unhappy, miser-era-erum

unless, nisi

unlike, dissimilis-e

unskilled, imperītus-a-um (cf. par. 19 Note)

unwilling (be), nōlō, nōlle, nōluī, ——————

unworthy, indignus-a-um (cf. par. 38a)

urge, hortor, 1

use, ūtor-ī, ūsus (cf. par. 35a)

useful, ūtilis-e; ūsuī (cf. par. 18)

V

valley, vallēs-is, f.

Veii, Veiī-ōrum, m.

village, vīcus-ī, m.

voice, vōx, vōcis, f.

W

wage, gerō-ere, gessī, gestus

wait, moror, 1

wall, mūrus-ī, m. moenia-ium, n. (walls of a city)

wander, vagor, 1

want, cupiō-ere, cupīvī, cupītus; volō, velle, voluī, ———

war, bellum-ī, n.

warn, moneō-ēre, monuī, monitus

water, aqua-ae, f.

we, nōs

weapon, tēlum-ī, n.

wear out, cōnficiō-ere, cōnfeci, cōnfectus

weep, fleō-ēre, flēvī, flētus

what, quī, quae, quod (interrog. adj.); quid (interrog. pronoun)

when, cum

where, ubi (in what place); quō (to what place)

whether, num

whether . . . or, utrum . . . an

whether . . . or not, utrum . . . necne

which, quī, quae, quod (relative pronoun); quī, quae, quod (interrog. adj.); uter-tra-trum (which of two)

while, cum

who, quī, quae, quod (relative pronoun); quis (interrog. pronoun)

whole, tōtus-a-um

why, cūr

wide, lātus-a-um

wife, uxor-ōris, f.

win, superō, 1

wind, ventus-ī, m.

wine, vīnum-ī, n.

winter, hiems, hiemis, f.

winter quarters, hīberna-ōrum, n.

wish, cupiō-ere, cupīvī, cupītus; volō, velle, voluī, ———

wish (not), nōlō, nōlle, nōluī, ———

with, cum (prep. w. abl.)

withstand, sustineō-ēre, sustinuī, sustentus

woman, fēmina-ae, f.

woods, silvae-ārum, f.

work, opus-eris, n.

work, labōrō, 1

worthy, dignus-a-um (cf. par 38a)

wound, vulnus-eris, n.

wound, vulnerō, 1

wreck, frangō-ere, frēgī, frāctus

wretched, miser-era-erum

write, scrībō-ere, scrīpsī, scrīptus

Y

year, annus-ī, m.

yet (not), nōndum

you, tu; vōs

young, iuvenis-is

young man, adulēscēns-entis, m.

your, yours, tuus-a-um; vester-tra-trum

Z

zeal, studium-ī, n.